Great
Isaac

Bimini
Islands

Gun Cay

Cat Cays

Ocean Cay

Riding
Rocks

367

Orange Cay

B

A

H

A

M

A

S

Andros Island

GREAT BAHAMA BANK

33

1300

700

33

1390

1100

25°N

75°W

☆Nassau

Bimini Islands

North Rock

North
Bimini

East
Bimini

Porgy Bay

Bailey Town

Alice Town

Middle Cay

South
Bimini

Rabbit
Keys

0   4mi

0   4km

W9-BCK-567

Old Bahama Channel

275

434

Cayo Guillermo

Cayo Coco

Cayo Paredón

Cayo Megano

Cayo Cruz

Cayo
Lobos

Cayo Confites

Cayo Romano

Bahía de Jigüey

220

1

600

1

800

2

2

7

33

1390

1100

1575

1470

1345

Cayo Sabinal

Morón

B

ego de Ávila

Florida

Vertientes

Minas

⊙Camagüey

Nuevitas

Golfo de
Ana María

A

Puerto Padre

Gibara

Banes

⊙Las Tunas

Holguín⊙

Bahía de Nipe

Moa

Santa Cruz
del Sur

Mayarí

Golfo de
Guacanayabo

Manzanillo

Bayamo⊙

Guantánamo⊙

Baracoa

nes de la Reina

Niquero

⊙Santiago
de Cuba

Bahía de Guantánamo

Windward Passage

33

THIS BOOK BELONGS TO

_____

HEMINGWAY IN CUBA

HILARY HEMINGWAY & CARLENE BRENNEN

RUGGED LAND | 276 CANAL STREET · FIFTH FLOOR · NEW YORK · NY · 10013 · USA

RuggedLand

Published by Rugged Land, LLC

276 CANAL STREET • FIFTH FLOOR • NEW YORK CITY • NY 10013 • USA
RUGGED LAND and colophon are trademarks of Rugged Land, LLC.

PUBLISHER'S CATALOGING-IN-PUBLICATION
(PROVIDED BY QUALITY BOOKS, INC.)

Hemingway, Hilary.
Hemingway in Cuba / Hilary Hemingway and Carlene Brennen.
p. cm.
Includes bibliographical references.
LCCN 2002117828
ISBN 159071010X

1. Hemingway, Ernest, 1899-1961--Homes and haunts--Cuba.
2. Authors, American--20th century--Biography.
3. Authors, American--Homes and haunts--Cuba.
4. Americans--Cuba--Biography. I. Brennen, Carlene.
II. Title.

PS3515.E37Z61715 2003   813'.52
QBI03-200043

Book Design by
HSU + ASSOCIATES

Maps by
BOB PRATT

RUGGED LAND WEBSITE ADDRESS:WWW.RUGGEDLAND.COM
JUNE 2003
1 3 5 7 9 10 8 6 4 2
First Edition

DEDICATION

To Jeffry P. Lindsay and Susan Lesko

To Terry Brennen and Shamie Kelly

TABLE OF CONTENTS

HE WROTE AS DARINGLY AS HE LIVED.

MAX PERKINS, ON ERNEST HEMINGWAY

HAVANA HARBOR

CHAPTER № 01

Ernest Hemingway first set foot on Cuban soil in 1928, but the two-day layover in Havana was not enough to experience all that Cuba had to offer. In the summer of 1932, Papa returned with two of his Key West friends for the annual marlin run. Their two-week fishing trip turned into a two-month adventure. It was on this excursion that Hemingway was introduced to Cuba, and Cuba to Ernest Hemingway.

Papa had chartered a low-slung thirty-four-foot cabin cruiser, the *Anita*, from his friend, a bootlegger named Joe Russell. Ernest had first met him in Key West while cashing his royalty check at Russell's speakeasy, and nicknamed him "Josie." Russell had made more than 150 rum-running trips from Key West to Cuba during the Prohibition years. In doing so, he had learned to read the Cuban coastline at night by the lights on shore, and still preferred to make his crossings under cloak of darkness. Russell's mate, an old Conch rummy named Joe Lowe, knew more about boats than fishing, so once they reached shore, Russell hired a black Cuban to rig baits.

Key West friend Joe Russell (center) introduced Hemingway (right) to marlin fishing in Cuba

It was without question the start of a superb marlin season. The commercial fishermen had already begun to bring in record numbers of white marlin. The fishing smacks normally tied to the Casablanca dock were already out before the sun peeked through the gray sky. Russell and Hemingway took their time, eating breakfast at the Pearl Café across from the San Francisco Wharf where Russell kept his boat.

Soon they headed out of the harbor, and a rainsquall passed overhead, beating down the waves to a light swell. The *Anita*'s bow cut through the waves with ease as they headed south away from the old fortress El Morro. A large frigate bird followed the boat out to sea, its black wings and V-shaped tail outlined against the pale sky.

"Man-o'-war." Hemingway pointed up at the bird.

The Cuban glanced up and said in Spanish, "Good luck, very good luck."

Ernest watched how the Cuban ran the hook through the mouth of the bait and out the gill, how he pushed the barbed point through the flank of meat so that it would not spin on the line, but would troll flat. The Cuban's fingers had withered from years of soaking in brine, but still tied baits with remarkable speed. By the time the *Anita* was clear of the harbor, the Cuban had prepared a half dozen baits, each finished with the mouth tied shut, with leader wire and the sides of the bait cut into strips to give off more scent in the water. He looked up from the bucket where he had laid the baits in water with their leaders neatly coiled. Ernest saw fatigue in the lines of the Cuban's face.

"What's the matter, my friend?" Papa asked in Spanish.

The Cuban shook off his expression and smirked. "The ladies," he answered, giving a twist of his hips doing the rumba. Ernest laughed and patted his back.

The *Anita* did not have outriggers, so the four fishing lines fed out from the tip of the rods like long trailing whips. Directly off the stern two wooden teasers trolled, zigzagging through the water and churning up a white foam trail.

"Josie," Ernest said to Russell, "we will find fish today. Too bloody marvelous out here to have no luck."

Russell smiled and called to Lowe at the helm, "Come about and head her out toward the Gulf Stream." He turned back to Ernest and pointed at the white dome above the Havana skyline. "Look, Papa, the twin to our Capitol in Washington. But the Cubans built theirs a few feet taller."

"Apparently size does matter," Ernest added.

El Capitolio, a close replica of the Capitol building in Washington.

The Cuban had lain down under the wooden canopy of the cabin. Papa turned to Russell and said under his breath, "Too much dancing for his own damn good." The men turned and stared out at the trailing baits. The sun turned the ocean's surface into a sea of diamonds.

Russell was first to spot the silver-purple bulk moving fast underwater, its wide pectoral fins spread like birds' wings. The billfish cut out of the wave, revealing its long dark and silver body. The swinging bill smacked at the water beside the trolling bait.

"Fish up. Port line. Fish up! Lowe, get those goddamn lines in," yelled Russell. Ernest reached for the second port rod and pulled it out of the holder in the gunnel.

Lowe glanced back; the Cuban was still fast asleep. He slowed the *Anita* down.

"Wake up, we got fish up." He kicked the Cuban's arm. The Cuban shook his head, looking up at Lowe blurry-eyed.

"Take the helm," Lowe said and pulled the Cuban up to the wheel.

Ernest held the heavy rod and dropped back the line as he stood braced against the boat's transom. There was no secured fighting chair on board the *Anita*; Ernest fought the fish standing up and Russell clipped a harness on him. Lowe quickly cleared the first of the lines from the other three reels. "Looks kinda small for a marlin," he said, nodding out toward the water.

"What do you know," Papa said to the old rummy.

"Lowe doesn't know anything." Russell countered. "Can't tell a damn thing till the fish is in the boat."

Ernest pressed his thumbs on the wooden wedge to slow the spool of line.

"Get ready, Papa," Russell coached. "Strike when I tell you... and strike hard three times... now!"

Ernest locked the gear and jerked the heavy rod back hard. He hit it three times fast, setting the steel hook into the jawbone. Ernest then bucked forward suddenly, and Russell grabbed Hemingway's belt before he was pulled over the transom's edge.

"What a great fish," Papa said with a grin. He braced his feet for leverage and felt a sharp pain in his knee, an old war wound. Both arms straining, he pulled back and felt the full weight of the fish on the line. The rod bent double as he lifted again. He waited a moment, watching the fish take the line out steadily, at will. "When the fish stops his first run," Russell said, "give him all you've got."

Ernest lowered the rod and reeled. It was a small victory, just a few feet of line. He gave another pull, and suddenly the line slacked as the marlin rose up out of the water, its eight-foot-long body rising higher until only the lower tip of the crescent tail touched the water's surface. Its iridescent blue and black dotted sail stretched out like a tight canvas, the fish moved across the waves with the grace of a dancer, arching its body. The spray gave off a brief but brilliant rainbow, red, blue and green.

"Papa," Russell cheered. "That's a hell of a fine sail."

"Six days of nothing," Papa agreed. "Now a possible world record. You plan this, Josie?"

"Hell yes." Russell laughed and turned to look toward the bow. The Cuban had fallen asleep holding the ship's wheel. Russell yelled at Lowe to go wake him.

From left to right: Hemingway, mate Carlos Gutierrez, Russell and mate Joe Lowe on the Anita.

Ernest wrote about this trip to his good friend John Dos Passos: "Well you played it wrong not to make this trip…. Have caught 19 Marlin Swordfish and 3 sailfish (one 8 feet 9 inches). Been feeding the whole water front…. can't get a son of a bitch down here—am feeling alone now with Joe holding the other rod and an insane night life jig to steer—goes to sleep while steering—goes to sleep minute he hits the boat. Spends the dough he makes every night on night life."

Havana harbor.

They got back to the San Francisco Wharf late that afternoon, and Hemingway and Russell headed down the street to Donovan's Bar. Russell, who was married and had three children, lived a quiet life in Key West. Captaining a fishing boat had been the perfect cover for a second career as a bootlegger and he did little to raise suspicions in Key West. But in Havana, Russell transformed from a loving husband and father into a rum-running pirate.

"Listen, Josie," Ernest began, "you teaching me this marlin thing—I can't thank you enough, but I want to know more about the Hoover Gold." Thanks to Prohibition, liquor was as good as gold.

"Funny you should ask," Russell said as they rounded the next corner, heading into a seedier neighborhood along the harbor. "I've got some business to take care of—wasn't gonna involve you, but now, with you wanting to know and all…."

"Thanks, Josie," Hemingway said. "I'll keep it on the QT."

Russell led Ernest into Donovan's Bar, a dirty little place not far from the wharf. It was a good place to grab a cold beer, and a place where deals were made involving flesh and alcohol. A thin man greeted Russell from behind the bar. Sliding past another, taller Cuban behind the counter, the bartender led Hemingway and Russell past an assortment of sailors, fishermen and prostitutes. In the back past the storage room was another locked door, and the bartender used his key to open it.

Stepping through, Russell and Hemingway entered the room and found an old Cuban working on a set of books and ledgers. Sitting beside him was a pretty mulatto prostitute.

"My friend," the Cuban said, standing to greet Russell with a handshake. "How is it for you Yankees?" He then turned and shook hands with Ernest.

"Thirsty. We're getting damn thirsty over there," Russell said. He took his shopping list from his shirt pocket and passed it over to the man, who studied it for a moment.

"I can get what you need," the Cuban said, looking up. "No problem—we have everything you want. Tell me—" He paused. "Have you ever considered any other items?"

"Like what?" Russell asked.

"I know of some people who would like to visit your country. They pay well."

"No," Russell said unblinking.

"You're sure?" The old man asked.

"No." Russell said. "I won't carry anything that can talk." His tone was resolute.

"Very well," said the old man. "I will fill your list as you ask." He then rose to his feet and shook their hands again.

"A pleasure," Hemingway told him, and then nodded to the prostitute, who smiled.

Ernest would later use this adventure with Russell to create his protagonist Harry Morgan, who is asked by three wealthy Cubans to smuggle them across to Key West on Morgan's boat, the *Queen Conch*. Morgan decides against smuggling the men for fear of losing his boat if caught, a stand that Russell is said to have taken.

"Listen," I said. "I told you I didn't carry anything that *can* talk. Sacked liquor can't talk. Demijohns can't talk. There's other things that can't talk. Men can talk."

TO HAVE AND HAVE NOT

At that time, hundreds of young Cubans were part of a revolutionary group called ABC, with the goal to oust Cuba's president, General Gerardo Machado. But days before they succeeded, many were hunted down and killed. Some were successful in getting smuggled off the island. Others died at the hands of the government-ordered *partidos de la porra*, or death squads.

The atmosphere was so unnerving that Ernest asked his editor at Scribners, Max Perkins, to send a letter stating that Hemingway was in Cuba on official business writing a story about the migratory fish of the Gulf Stream. Ernest hoped this would get him out of a jam in the event he ran into trouble. The Machado agents were cracking down not only on students, but also on Americans whom they suspected of aiding the revolutionaries. But as it turned out, it was not Ernest's life that was in danger.

Hemingway stayed at Hotel Ambos Mundos during his visits from 1932 to 1939.

HOTEL AMBOS MUNDOS AND SAN FRANCISCO WHARF

CHAPTER № 02

On August 4, 1933, Ernest Hemingway, his eldest son Jack ("Bumby,") his middle son Patrick ("Mouse,") his wife Pauline and her sister, Jinny Pfeiffer, returned to Havana where they would sail on the ship *Reina de la Pacífica* to Spain. Ernest had spent most of that summer fishing and writing; he planned to spend the next two months attending bullfights in Spain before visiting Paris to deliver Bumby to his mother, Hadley. During the three-day layover in Havana, the Hemingways and Jinny Pfeiffer stayed at the Hotel Ambos Mundos.

On the evening before they were to set sail, Pauline sat in room 511 at the Ambos Mundos, waiting for her husband and sons to return. A loud crack sounded, followed by a boom. Pauline hurried to the window, expecting to see some kind of riot in the street, but saw only a thunderhead in the distance moving across the water.

You worry too much, Pauline chided herself; but over two hours had passed since Ernest had taken his sons down to the dock to see the ship. She glanced down at the empty street below; the daily crowds of Cubans hurrying to and from work had disappeared. A general strike had gripped the city for over a week, meaning no postal or food deliveries, and there had been reports of fighting in the streets between the leftist revolutionaries and government agents.

Pauline looked up again at the rainsquall moving into the mouth of Havana harbor. As the gray curtain of rain swept heavily over the old fortress, El Morro disappeared from sight. There was a knock at the door before it swung open.

"They're not back yet?"

Jinny Pfeiffer stepped into her sister's room. Pauline turned and tried to sound nonchalant. "The ship just got

Pauline and Ernest Hemingway.

in. Who knows, Papa probably made friends with the captain by now and they're teaching Bumby how to steer the ship."

A loud pop, pop, pop rang out from the streets.

Pauline breathed in sharply. "Is that gunfire?"

"Gunfire? Where?" Jinny said, joining her sister at the window. After a moment she added. "I don't see anything."

"Probably the storm," said Pauline. She glanced at her watch, exasperated. "We'll never make dinner. Honestly, he loses track of time."

"Do you think this is all right for dinner?" Jinny asked, smoothing down her silk white blouse and matching pants.

"It's fine," Pauline answered absently and reached for her purse. "Come on, let's find Ernest."

Ducking out of the corner door of the hotel, Pauline and Jinny walked along Calle Obispo. The small open-air markets along the street that were packed during the earlier part of the summer were now closed and abandoned. The street was quiet, with only three or four people in view farther down the block. They walked hurriedly, ducking in and out of doorways as if there were a hard rain falling, but the rain had not yet reached Old Havana.

Pauline Hemingway standing at the window of her room at Hotel Ambos Mundos.

Pauline and Jinny came to the corner of Calle Oficios and turned toward the docks. A black car suddenly raced by, narrowly missing them as they crossed the street. Pauline pushed Jinny into the nearest doorway, and they heard a scream a block away as the car ran up against a building wall and hit a young man. The women watched aghast as the car continued chasing four other young men, who were running for their lives. One reached up and grabbed the wrought-iron bars over a window, pulling himself to the second- and then the third-story balcony. The car slowed down; a man leaned out the window, aimed and fired. The young man dropped from the third floor like a rag doll; his death bought his friends enough time to make the next corner. Jinny and Pauline held on to each other, horrified. The shooter slipped back into his seat and the car raced off.

"President Machado's doing," Pauline whispered. "He's killing this country."

They waited a few minutes. As people slowly returned to the street, they continued toward the wharf. A woman screamed. Pauline and Jinny turned to see the crowds gather over the dead boy.

"Oh God, get us off this island," said Jinny, picking up her pace.

They were within half a block of the San Francisco Wharf; they could see the old bell towers of the cathedral looming ahead. As they came around the church building they saw the *Reina de la Pacífica* at the pier. "Tomorrow we'll be safe at sea," Pauline reassured her sister.

But they were not safe. As they walked toward the wharf, three teenage boys hunched down behind a truck at the edge of the square. They talked among themselves, and then made a mad dash toward the old cathedral as Pauline and Jinny turned the corner.

Pauline suddenly felt pieces of the cathedral wall sting her arm and leg, as shots rang out over the square. Jinny saw the first young man fall into the fountain and screamed for her sister to get down. In another moment, the shootout was over and the three boys were dead.

One of the boys was spread out on the sidewalk, face down, just outside the big window that was smashed. The other two were behind one of the Tropical beer ice wagons that was stopped in front of the Cunard bar next door. One of the ice-wagon horses was down in the harness, kicking, and the other was plunging his head off.

One of the boys shot from the rear corner of the wagon and it ricocheted off the sidewalk. The nigger with the Tommy gun got his face almost into the street and gave the back of the wagon a burst from underneath and sure enough one came down, falling toward the sidewalk with his head above the curb.

TO HAVE AND HAVE NOT

Ernest had been across the square in the Pearl Café, buying Bumby and Mouse cold sodas before walking back to the hotel. When the first shots rang out, he was one of the first on the scene.

Ernest later told Max Perkins, "Saw everything that happened—No not everything—but what one person could see—keeping in the streets when supposed to be fatal and with my customary fragility or whatever G. Stein called it had no marks—Pauline and Jinny both fired on in the streets—food etc cut off for 3 days"

The Fountain of the Lions is situated in the middle of Plaza de San Francisco, between the Basílica Menor de San Francisco de Asís, known simply as the Old Cathedral, and San Francisco Wharf.

Castillo de los Tres Santos Reyes Magos del Morro, or the Castle of the Three Holy Kings.

Built by Spain in the 16th century with coral blocks taken off the coastal reef, El Morro was designed to protect Havana Harbor from pirates.

FISHING OFF EL MORRO CASTLE

CHAPTER № 03

In the *Esquire* article "Marlin off the Morro: A Cuban Letter," Ernest tells how he first met Captain Carlos Gutierrez when they were both stormbound in the Dry Tortugas. Though they would spend only a few short seasons fishing off Havana together, Ernest greatly respected Gutierrez and his extensive knowledge of billfishing: "The other man on board is the best marlin and swordfisherman around Cuba, Carlos Gutierrez.... He can, literally, gaff a dolphin through the head back-handed and he has studied the habits of the marlin since he first went fishing for them as a boy of twelve with his father."

In the summer of 1933, Russell motored the *Anita* to the Casablanca docks just down from El Morro Castle. They needed to hire a full time mate. On the dock where the fishermen came to sell their catch, Ernest caught up with Gutierrez and bought the fifty-four-year-old Cuban a drink. Don Carlos, as Ernest came to call him affectionately, held the record among the commercial Cuban fishermen for boating the most marlin and swordfish. By the end of the drink, Carlos had signed on as mate.

Gutierrez taught Ernest and Russell how to set the lines at varying depths for marlin, how to safely gaff and bring a big marlin on board. With Don Carlos's help Ernest landed a whopping fifty-two marlin that summer, averaging a fish a day for the entire stay. Everything, the skill of the crew and Ernest's knowledge of billfishing, came together the day he brought in the 468-pound blue marlin off El Morro Castle.

Carlos Gutierrez aboard the Anita. By the end of the summer, Hemingway had boated fifty-two marlin with his help.

Carlos ran bait on the first flat line back. Lowe sat on the *Anita*'s cabin roof looking out over the water for any signs of billfish. Russell had the helm. Ernest kept his eyes trained on the trailing bait.

"You know, Don Carlos," Ernest said in Spanish, "I am beginning to think there are only four different ways these damn billfish hit a bait."

"*Sí*, Ernesto?"

"In starvation, and in belligerence," he paused then added, "amusement, and with a certain amount of apathy."

"*Sí*, Ernesto," Carlos laughed and agreed. He pushed another steel hook through a small slit in the belly of the bait. The eye of the hook came out the bait's mouth, where he tied it to the double leader of the second flat line.

"Now a truly starving fish is hard to muck up. You can't miss seeing him in the water, because when he crashes the bait, his bill, head, dorsal and tail, are all splashing on the surface. So you just slack some line and set the goddamn hook."

"*Sí*, Ernesto," Carlos said again and ran the flat line out over the stern, keeping his thumb on the spinning spool so it would not backlash.

"And what of the belligerent fish? Well, hell, he's a mystery. You've seen him. The one that races up from the deep and whacks the bait. He hits with such force, the bait's ruined, even if the fish doesn't eat it. But to catch him, ahhh. There's only one way–hit him hard as he crashes it. Timing is crucial. If you strike before he does, the bait is pulled out of his mouth. If you wait, he will drop it."

"*Sí*," Carlos chuckled. "I have seen this one too many times."

"Now the trickier one. I call it the amused marlin. These illegitimates have eaten plenty. Hell, they don't really want the bait at all. They chase it, smack it, take it in their mouth and spit it out. The only way to hook them is to race the skiff, or jump the bait with your line. Then it becomes a game to these fish. They will charge the bait with the frustration of a mad dog whose fence you have crossed."

"*Sí*, Ernesto. Very troubling."

"No, Don Carlos, the most troubling is the bloody apathetic fish," Ernest said, helping Carlos put the next rod into the port gunnel. "The apathetic ones follow the baits for miles, zigzagging behind, looking it over, but never close enough to strike. These fish you could shoot, and I've been plenty tempted, because you'll never catch them on rod and reel."

"Ernesto, I think you now understand billfish better than any man alive."

"No, billfish are still very much a mystery. But someday, I think we will know them. There is much still to learn, my friend."

Ernest wrote down his observations. He always kept a ship's log, recording not only what was caught, but how it was caught. He would work these notes into his *Esquire* stories. He wanted the readers to understand deep-sea fishing, to feel as though they were on board fishing with him: "The marlin hit a trolled bait in four different ways. First, with

Hemingway, flanked by Carlos (left) and Russell (right), proudly displays his 468-pound blue marlin.

Carlos Gutierrez and Hemingway on board the Anita.

hunger, again with anger, then simply playfully, last with indifference."

With only the first three lines in the water, Lowe suddenly stomped his foot on the cabin roof. "Fish up. Fish up. Marlin. Starboard line."

Ernest took the rod and slacked out the line from the reel perfectly. He kept his eyes on the whole great purple length of the marlin, admiring the black sword smashing the bait, the dorsal fin cutting the water, the wide shoulders being pushed above by the powerful tail.

The entire waterfront turns out for Hemingway's catch.

"A fine starving fish," Papa declared and let out more line, so the beast would take the bait well into its mouth. When the jaw shut and the fish disappeared, he was ready. He glanced at his rod tip to make sure the line wasn't foul, then struck hard. He hit it again, twice more to set the hook deep into the fish's jawbone. Then he felt the absolute power of this fish, the bent rod, the gimbal belt pushed hard against the muscles in his flat stomach; then off the stern, the calm of the ocean broke as the marlin launched itself. Rising up, its wet, dark body hung above the water for an impossibly long moment. It shook its head and body, throwing off two remoras that hung to its underside. But it had no chance to fling the sharp hook imbedded in the corner of its mouth and the big blue smashed back into water. White spray churned up and he launched himself three more times, greyhounding across the surface followed by the zinging scream of the fishing line.

"Look at him. Like a racehorse." Russell laughed.

"Yes, as strong as a horse. And like a horse I will break his spirit," Ernest growled as he continued to pump and reel the line steadily. "I will treat him as a horse. Lead him, convince him, until he knows I am in charge."

"*Sí*, Ernesto. That's it."

The fish came up and jumped eleven more times, his silver belly flickering in the sunlight like a wet mirror. Ernest continued to pump and reel, trying to get the belly out of the line before the fish snapped it. But in the series of leaps, Ernest watched the line melt off the reel. Then for reasons unknown, the marlin turned back toward the *Anita*.

"Ernesto, he is coming in."

"I see that, Don Carlos," Ernest said, reeling fast now. "Josie, give her some juice. I don't want... oh shit." Ernest's voice trailed off as he watched the great fish suddenly disappear under the water. The line raced toward the hull at a tremendous speed.

"He's changing sides," Ernest yelled. "Neutral, Joe. Carlos, get this damn harness off me." The Cuban worked quickly to release the harness and rod from the gimbal belt. Papa kept reeling, as the large marlin swam under the boat. The *Anita* already had eight bills broken off in her hull and the boat was beginning to take on water. Ernest loosened the drag, and ripped line out with his fingers. He turned to Carlos. "Do you see him?"

The Cuban waited a moment until he was sure. "Yes," he answered, pointing to the dark shadow surfacing. "He's there now. He's on the other side of the boat."

Here was the problem: the fishing line was on the port side of the boat, crossing the bottom and resurfacing on the starboard side where the fish now rested on the surface. If the line touched the boat's hull, it would snap.

"What are we going to do, Ernesto?"

"Hang on to me, Carlos," Ernest said. He bent over the port gunnel, dipping the rod tip deep into the water. "I'm going... to try to pass the line... under the boat... missing, I hope... the prop and rudder." The Cuban held onto Ernest's waist as he leaned over the gunnel and walked the line aft toward the stern. "God... tell me... if he moves."

Ernest's luck held. The fish came to the surface as Papa successfully passed the line safely to the starboard.

"Good, very good," Carlos said approvingly.

"We'll see, it might have nicked the line," Ernest said, catching his breath before pumping and reeling again. He fought this round leaning against the transom in the full midday heat. A small crowd gathered around the Morro's lighthouse; the lighthouse keeper watched from his window. They watched as Carlos doused Papa twice with buckets of seawater to keep him cooled off, and as he lunged for him to counter the weight of the fish pulling him overboard.

At last, the great fish was brought alongside and Ernest took the double leader in his hands while Carlos leaned out and gaffed the fish. The big blue shuddered against the side of the hull, its bill smacking and scratching the *Anita*'s planking.

"The hell you do," Papa growled and leaned over with the wooden persuader to whack the fish squarely on the forehead. "Huh," he said, looking the fish over, "he might just go five hundred pounds."

"Ah," said Carlos, "this will be the bread of my children."

The fished weighed in at 468 pounds, twelve feet and eight inches long. By the end of summer Ernest wrote Arnold Gingrich, editor of *Esquire*: "Have 39 Marlin swordfish now. Have all the dope for the Cuban letter and will write it the first day that the wind is bad for fishing."

The lighthouse of El Morro.

Carlos Gutierrez was not as well known as Hemingway's other first mate, Gregorio Fuentes, but his impact on Ernest extended beyond teaching him about billfishing. Ernest himself credited the old Cuban with billfish stories that he used in his *Esquire* letter published April 1936, "On The Blue Water: A Gulf Stream Letter":

"Another time an old man fishing alone in a skiff out of Cabanas hooked a great marlin that, on the heavy sashcord handline, pulled the skiff far out to sea. Two days later the old man was picked up by fishermen sixty miles to the eastward, the head and forward part of the marlin lashed alongside. What was left of the fish, less than half, weighed eight hundred pounds. The old man had stayed with him a day, a night, a day and another night while the fish swam deep and pulled the boat. When he had come up the old man had pulled the boat up on him and harpooned him. Lashed alongside the sharks had hit him and the old man had fought them out alone in the Gulf Stream in a skiff, clubbing them, stabbing at them, lunging at them with an oar until he was exhausted and the sharks had eaten all that they could hold. He was crying in the boat when the fishermen picked him up, half crazy from his loss, and the sharks were still circling the boat."

Clearly this was the genesis of what eventually developed into *The Old Man and the Sea*. Ernest wanted to get all the details right, and he outlined the story in February 1939 to his editor Max Perkins: "One about the old commercial fisherman who fought the swordfish all alone in his skiff for 4 days and four nights and the sharks finally eating it after he had it alongside and could not get it into the boat. That's a wonderful story of the Cuban coast. I'm going out with old Carlos in his skiff so as to get it all right. Everything he does and everything he thinks in all that long fight with the boat out of sight of all the other boats all alone on the sea. It's a great story if I can get right. One that would make the book."

It did and won Hemingway the Pulitzer Prize in 1953, followed the next year by the announcement heard over the *Pilar*'s radio: "...For his mastery of the art of narrative, most recently demonstrated in *The Old Man and the Sea*, and for the influence that he has exerted on contemporary style, the 1954 Nobel Prize for Literature has been awarded to Ernest Hemingway." ▨

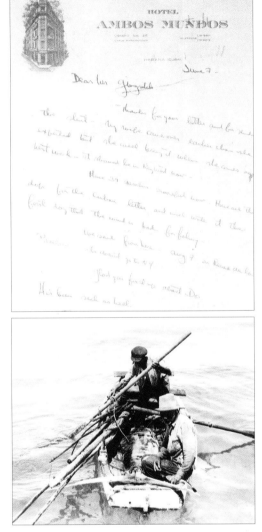

Hemingway's letter to Arnold Gingrich, on hotel stationery.

Cuban fishermen, Hemingway's inspiration for
The Old Man and the Sea.

Carlos Gutierrez and Jane Mason.

JANE MASON

CHAPTER № 04

On the evening of May 23, 1933, Ernest returned to his hotel room at the Ambos Mundos after greeting his five-year-old son Patrick (Mouse) and nanny Ada Stern. They had crossed over from Key West on the ferry and were to stay as houseguests of Grant and Jane Mason, joining Hemingway's ten-year-old Jack (Bumby), who was already staying there. They lived in a large estate west of Havana in the suburb of Jaimanitas with their three-year-old son, Anthony, and a backyard menagerie that included a honey bear, a monkey, a fox, peacocks, flamingoes, parrots, pigeons and three large dogs. To maintain order in this expansive residence, the Masons employed a Haitian houseman, a Chinese cook, an Italian butler, a German gardener, and a Cuban chauffeur. Earlier on in the season, Ernest had welcomed the company of both Grant and Jane Mason on board the *Anita*, and fished with Charles Thompson and Pauline's uncle Gus the last two weeks of April. His flirting with Jane seemed harmless, but Pauline had noticed his attraction to the young beauty and made mention of Mrs. Mason in a letter to Ernest: "Am having large nose, imperfect lips, protruding ears and warts and moles all taken off before coming to Cuba. Thought I'd better, Mrs. Mason and those Cuban women are so lovely."

In the quiet of his hotel room, Ernest set down his thoughts on paper. He had been invited by Arnold Gingrich to write for a new men's magazine he was publishing, though Ernest thought the name of the magazine, *Esquire,* would never fly. It smacked of snobbery, but Hemingway was warming up to the idea of getting back to journalism. He loved explaining to others how to go about doing something, and in that way he was a natural teacher. Sitting at the desk with a notepad, he thought about how he would explain marlin fishing to these gentlemen readers. He made notes about his own schedule: a quick shower, dressing in comfortable clothes, heading down to the café for breakfast. He likened the physical demands of deep-sea fishing to that of a boxer in training—you didn't fill your stomach before the workout.

The Mason estate.

Though Pauline (right) likely noticed her husband's attentions to Mrs. Mason, she showed no outward change in her manner toward Jane (right).

Pulling the rod back, then cranking the reel was the equivalent of doing a thousand sit-ups, only with the arms being pulled hard until they seemed ready to snap. He wrote in his notes, simple diet. Start with a slice of Cuban bread and a cold glass of milk and a glass of mineral water. The way the fish had been running, they would feed in the morning and late afternoon, leaving noon for the fisherman to have a good solid lunch.

The ledge outside Ernest's window at Ambos Mundos measured two and a half feet wide, ample space for Jane Mason's daredevil stunt.

As he jotted down his thoughts, Papa heard a tapping on his bedroom window, light as the pecking of a bird, but curiously rhythmic. He went over to the tall, shuttered window and pulled it open. He saw a pink scarf and a flutter of blond hair as Jane Mason smiled and bent down. "Jane, my beauty! What are you up to?" Ernest asked as Mason climbed in through the window from the two-and-half-foot-wide brick ledge that ran from her room next door.

"Oh, I was just in the neighborhood and thought I'd surprise you," the blonde answered, deftly slipping under Papa's arm and into his room. "I thought you might like to hear some of my ideas about your upcoming safari."

Ernest closed the wooden shutters and turned to find that Jane had stretched out across his bed. He moved toward her. "Tell me of your thoughts, daughter."

Though the specifics of their love affair remain for the most part unpublished, this passage of *To Have and Have Not* indicates how Ernest drew upon the affair for inspiration, perhaps even betraying his own fear of getting caught in the act:

That afternoon she had not seen him as the door opened. She had not seen anything but the white ceiling with its cake-frosting modeling of cupids, doves and scroll work that the light from the open door suddenly made clear.

Richard Gordon had turned his head and seen him, standing heavy and bearded in the doorway.

"Don't stop," Helène had said. "Please don't stop." Her bright hair was spread over the pillow.

But Richard Gordon had stopped and his head was still turned, staring.

"Don't mind him. Don't mind anything. Don't you see you can't stop now?" the woman had said in desperate urgency.

The bearded man had closed the door softly. He was smiling.

"What's the matter, darling?" Helène Bradley had asked, now in the darkness again.

"I must go."

TO HAVE AND HAVE NOT

The next day, Ernest went out fishing again on board the *Anita* with Russell and first mate Carlos Gutierrez, and Jane Mason took the children to visit friends at Finca Milagras. The children having been out in the sun all day, Jane chose to close the convertible top of her Chevrolet for the drive home. A simple decision, but one that ended up saving all of their lives.

According to the *Havana Post* of May 24, 1933, Jane Mason, her young son, Tony, and Ernest's sons Jack and Patrick escaped serious injury in what could easily have been a fatal accident. On the drive back along the lush greenery of the hills, they passed through the town of El Cano.

Just ahead, heading toward them, a bus pulled out to bypass a slow-moving truck, unaware of their oncoming car. "Oh my God," Jane screamed as she swerved off the paved road and slammed on her brakes. The bus passed without slowing and continued on its way.

Jane began to exhale, but the car slowly started to slide over the soft dirt shoulder. "Oh God, hold on," she gasped, before the car tipped over into the embankment. Instinctively, Jane grabbed the keys out of the ignition. Patrick held on to Tony, who hung on his mother. Jack put his hands up against the imploding roof to protect his head. Tony could see Bumby in the backseat doing a strange cartwheel as the car rolled over. The view from the front window changed abruptly from blue sky to the brown dirt of the newly dug embankment. Gathering momentum, the car turned over two more times, sliding and tipping before coming to a rest, upside down. The smell of gas burned in their nostrils and the back of their throats felt thick.

"We've got to get out of here," Jane said still clutching the steering wheel.

"Try the doors," Bumby suggested.

Jane could not get either of the bent door frames to open, but Jack reached up for the window handle and after several swift turns, the glass rose up like a drawbridge. "Mrs. Mason, we can get out here."

The younger boys wiggled through under the glass. The Cuban teenagers who had been playing baseball nearby lifted the door frame by using their baseball bat as leverage, while Jane and Bumby dug at the earth to expand the escape hole.

Finally Bumby wiggled through and Jane followed soon after. By the time all four had extracted themselves from the wreck, more help was on its way. A young male employee of Pan American Airlines ran down the hill to help, and a Cuban woman followed, calling out to the boys in Spanish. "Children, children, are you all right?"

That evening, the boys and Jane returned to the Mason estate without further incident, and Ernest came over as soon as he heard the news. The near miss eventually made its way into the international press, worrying Pauline, who was still in Key West, and even Ernest's mother, Grace, who was in Chicago. She later wrote: "We are all so shocked to read in the papers this morning of your near tragedy. God is so good to have spared their lives and kept them safe and sound."

This near tragedy and another car accident in 1947 involving Gregory and Patrick spawned another passage in *Islands in the Stream*. The mental anguish the character Thomas Hudson suffers on learning of the deaths of his sons eventually leads him down a path of self-destruction. Like Hemingway, Hudson can hardly bear it when his sons leave him at the end of each summer to return to their mother, and the car accident that takes their lives precipitates his own undoing:

"Yes," Thomas Hudson said. "It's going to be goddam lonely."

Thomas Hudson was unhappy as soon as the boys were gone. But he thought that was normal lonesomeness for them and he just kept on working. The end of a man's own world does not come as it does in one of the great paintings Mr. Bobby had outlined. It comes with one of the island boys bringing a radio message up the road from the local post office and saying, "Please sign on the detachable part of the envelope. We're sorry, Mr. Tom."

He took the radio form out and read it again. YOUR SONS DAVID AND ANDREW KILLED WITH THEIR MOTHER IN MOTOR ACCIDENT NEAR BIARRITZ ATTENDING TO EVERYTHING PENDING YOUR ARRIVAL DEEPEST SYMPATHY.

ISLANDS IN THE STREAM

Ernest's eldest son Bumby said of Jane Mason, "She was a beautiful moth drawn to Ernest's flame." Although Ernest had tried to keep his affair with Jane discreet, someone saw fit to write in the ships log of the *Anita*, "Ernest loves Jane." Ernest himself boasted of the spectacular feat she executed to get into his room and his bed. Known for her theatrics, Jane apparently thought nothing of stepping onto a narrow ledge fifty feet above ground to make a dramatic entrance.

On several occasions, Ernest and Jane enjoyed what they called "cross-country runs" in her small imported sports car. After an afternoon drinking double daiquiris at the Floridita, they had discovered the pure adrenaline rush that occurs when driving with the sole purpose of scaring the other passenger. Les Hemingway said that these cross-country runs were nothing more than games of chicken to see who could endure longer in the passenger seat before screaming, "Slow down" or "Watch out."

Originally La Florida, the Floridita became one of Hemingway's favorite haunts.

Jane later said that Ernest did not play fair; he not only had the double daiquiris but would also take his glasses off. With his severe nearsightedness, he really couldn't see how close to death they came.

But while Ernest was very much in love with Jane, he struggled to reconcile his feelings with the guilt of cheating with the wife of a friend and of violating his own personal code of conduct. He wrote to Max Perkins regarding his observation on the moral decline of marriage. "All women married to a wrong husband are bad luck for themselves and all their friends." Most likely he tried to rationalize the affair; perhaps Grant Mason neglected his wife for business matters, or maybe Jane had grown tired of being married to an older man. His frustration and discomfort with his role in the classic love triangle are evidenced in his short story "The Short Happy Life of Francis Macomber":

So she woke him when she came in, Wilson thought, looking at them both with his flat, cold eyes. Well, why doesn't he keep his wife where she belongs? What does he think I am, a bloody plaster saint? Let him keep her where she belongs. It's his own fault.

THE SHORT HAPPY LIFE
OF FRANCIS MACOMBER

In the story, the husband eventually builds up the courage to face down his wife's indiscretions, only to be shot accidentally by her. For Jane Mason, the ending of her story turned out quite differently.

The day after her car accident, Jane returned to the dock to go fishing with Hemingway. In the *Anita's* log, Ernest noted that Jane caught two large marlin. No simple feat for anyone, much less a woman who had just survived a car accident. But the luck of this Pond's face cream model ran out by evening.

Exactly what happened that evening remains unclear. It is quite possible that Grant may have confronted his wife about her affair with Hemingway and forbidden her to see him again. But plans had already been made for Jane to celebrate with Ernest her two-marlin catch at La Floridita. With Pauline safely away in Key West, Jane would not miss her date with Ernest, not willingly at least.

Jane Mason's second floor studio.

Some have suggested that what transpired next was an attempt at suicide, that heavily medicated with painkillers from the car accident, Jane Mason had jumped out of her window. A Cuban newspaper reported that Mason had been shot by revolutionaries and fell from her balcony window. Other biographers have reported that Jane fell from a hotel window in old Havana, or at Hemingway's home in Key West. But the incident did not happen at a hotel, or at Hemingway's home, or because Jane had been shot. There was no indication that their affair was waning, or that there was any other reason for her to entertain the idea of taking her own life. Contrary to all popular opinions, the whole event should be reclassified as an accident of the heart.

Eager for another date with Ernest, Jane Mason may have attempted to climb down secretly from the second-story window of her art studio, but slipped and fell to the ground, breaking her back. When Ernest visited her at Havana's Anglo-American Hospital, he tried to cheer her spirits by saying, "You know, Jane, I've never had a girl fall so hard for me."

Grant Mason later sent Jane to New York, where she underwent back surgery and months of physical therapy. A seven-inch scar from a spinal fusion served as a memento of a date with Hemingway that Jane was not able to keep.

According to *Esquire* editor Arnold Gingrich, who later married Jane, her affair with Hemingway lasted five years, ending when Jane introduced her new boyfriend, Richard Cooper, a millionaire playboy and big game hunter, to Hemingway in Bimini.

Ernest was quite upset that Jane had fallen in love with someone else. He expressed his jealousy and anger in "The Short Happy Life of Francis Macomber," using Jane and Grant Mason as models for Francis and Margot Macomber, and Richard Cooper for the safari guide Robert Wilson.

Ernest also wrote of Margot Macomber as having a perfect oval face that commanded five thousand dollars for endorsing a beauty product that she never used, an exact description of Jane's endorsement of Pond's face cream. The description left little doubt as to the character's connection to Jane Mason. Francis and Margot Macomber had been married for eleven years, corresponding exactly to the period of Grant and Jane Mason's marriage from 1927 to 1938. Hemingway sums up the failed Mason marriage in these two lines:

> They had a sound basis of union. Margot was too beautiful for Macomber to divorce her and Macomber had too much money for Margot ever to leave him. ⊠

THE SHORT HAPPY LIFE
OF FRANCIS MACOMBER

THE CIENTÍFICOS

CHAPTER № 05

In 1934, Hemingway wrote his friend John Dos Passos, "I am in training to be a naturalist." Now it may be difficult for many to think of Ernest Hemingway as a naturalist or conservationist, since it seemed he never met an animal he didn't want to kill. But back then, being a conservationist—in the tradition of Teddy Roosevelt—meant conserving animals today to have animals to hunt tomorrow. It meant understanding these animals, studying them in their natural habitat, analyzing their migration, feeding habits and physical changes over their life span. Further, it meant sharing that mystical bond between the hunter and the prey, the bond that Ernest wrote of so memorably in *The Old Man and the Sea*. The character Santiago speaks of his love and admiration for the great fish even as he is determined to kill it:

Hemingway shows off his marlin as friend Sidney Franklin (right) looks on.

"The fish is my friend too," he said aloud. "I have never seen or heard of such a fish. But I must kill him. I am glad we do not have to try to kill the stars."

Imagine if each day a man must try to kill the moon, he thought. The moon runs away. But imagine if a man each day should have to try to kill the sun? We were born lucky, he thought.

Then he was sorry for the great fish that had nothing to eat and his determination to kill him never relaxed in his sorrow for him. How many people will he feed, he thought. But are they worthy to eat him? No, of course not. There is no one worthy of eating him from the manner of his behaviour and his great dignity.

I do not understand these things, he thought. But it is good that we do not have to try to kill the sun or the moon or the stars. It is enough to live on the sea and kill our true brothers.

THE OLD MAN AND THE SEA

In 1934, Hemingway set out to prove himself a naturalist, not only with his notes on his first African safari, but in Cuba, where he made plans to study the marlin species. It began shortly after he took delivery of his first sports fishing boat, the *Pilar*. He had christened the modified 38-foot Wheeler with the secret name he had for Pauline during their affair while Hemingway was married to his first wife, Hadley. The *Pilar* was designed for the pursuit of deep-sea fishing. Ernest lowered the transom a foot and installed a roller bar so he and his crew had less work to lift the huge fish on board.

The crew of the Pilar weighs in their catch at the Casablanca docks.

Inside, the *Pilar* gleamed with varnished mahogany and the smell of fresh paint, Italian leather and gasoline. She carried three hundred gallons of gas and was powered by a 75-horsepower Chrysler for speed and a small 40-horsepower Lycoming for trolling. She also had a 1500-gallon water tank.

On her maiden voyage to Cuba, Ernest brought an additional one hundred gallons of gas in small drums stowed in the forward locker, and food provisions were placed back in the lockers around the dinette and under the mid-ship bunks. Papa's crew consisted of a young writer named Arnold Samuelson, who he had nicknamed Maestro or Mice for his ability to play the violin, and a seaman from the P&O steamship line, Charles Lunn. The seaman joined Ernest for the crossing, but once Hemingway cleared customs, Lunn returned to Key West.

For fishing in Cuban waters, Hemingway again hired Captain Carlos Gutierrez as first mate, and another Cuban named Juan to be the *Pilar*'s chief cook and backup helmsman. Ernest had Juan and Samuelson sleep on board the *Pilar* while she was moored in Havana Harbor, and Ernest and his guests stayed in town at Hotel Ambos Mundos.

Ernest entertained many guests over the three-month fishing season, but he was most pleased to meet the two gentlemen from the Philadelphia Academy of Natural History: Charles Cadwalader, the academy's director and biggest benefactor, and Henry Fowler, the Academy's chief ichthyologist. Fowler carried with him several boxes of measuring and sampling tools, and Cadwalader brought along a medium weight fishing rod and reel, more symbolic than practical.

Ernest smiled and took the rod on board and placed it next to his own heavier rods and reels. He also invited a Venezuelan sportsman, Lopez Mendez, to join them for the first day of fishing during the monthlong study.

In what became Hemingway's seventh *Esquire* article, "Out in the Stream: A Cuban Letter," Ernest wrote of the questions and observations raised with Cadwalader and Fowler. Why is it that mako sharks never eat hooked marlin, when clearly other sharks do? What purpose does the sail serve on a sailfish? What is it that drives marlin to swim against the current? And could the white, blue, black and stripe marlin all be variations of the same species? Just how big could they grow? Hemingway even wondered if there would be a law someday to stop big game fishing, since everyone had far too swell a time catching these fish for it to continue as is.

As they motored out of Havana Harbor, Cadwalader, who drank only mineral water, looked out at the change in the color of the Gulf Stream. "Hemingway, what are the chances we can gain a complete collection of these marlin fish?"

"Well, no promises, but last summer about this time, I landed seven in one day. That may not happen right away—the commercial fishermen say the big run hasn't yet begun."

"That's okay. Henry can pick up all kinds of specimens for the Academy. You know, in the seaweed—when things are slow."

Fowler turned to Ernest at the *Pilar*'s wheel, and nodded toward the net he was putting together. "We may find juveniles in the seaweed."

"My good Científicos, trust me, once we get into a marlin," said Papa, "old seaweed will fail to keep your interest. Henry, I want you to scientifically differentiate these species. There has been an awful lot of horseshit claimed, so once and for all tell us if it's the same animal or truly different ones."

"I'll do my best," Henry agreed, and then looked aft at Carlos running back the first of the baits. Mendez stood next to the old Cuban and talked while pointing at various buildings along the harbor's edge.

The *Pilar* headed south for half an hour. Ernest kept his eyes on the small bonito baits as they trailed in the water, kicking up white stripes against a blue sea. Maestro sat on the edge of the gunnel looking back at the ocean, his face white despite his sunburn.

"Yes, sir. We're going to raise some good fish today," Ernest cheered. He turned to Cadwalader. "The wind is picking up from the southwest, that always brings in the big ones."

The director nodded and asked, "How big?"

"Damn big," Papa answered.

"Care for a wager?" Cadwalader teased. "I'll buy dinner for you—or for that matter everyone on board, if we can land anything over four hundred pounds; smaller and you buy."

"Hmmm. Hell, I'll take that offer; Carlos, take the helm," Ernest said as his mate took over the wheel and then Ernest sat in his custom-built fighting chair. He kept his eyes fixed on the trailing baits and glaring blue water. Mendez grabbed one of the old wicker seats and pulled it up next to Ernest's right side. The men talked in Spanish for a moment, and then Ernest turned back to Cadwalader, who was standing in the shade of the cabin.

"Mendez here brings up a good point, " Ernest said to Cadwalader.

"How's that?" asked the director as he grabbed the other wicker chair and pulled it over to them.

"He said black marlin he's caught have all been old fish and female."

"So Ernest suggested," Mendez continued with his Venezuelan accent, "maybe like the jewfish the marlin might start out male and female, but as it matures—they turn female."

"Interesting theory," Cadwalader agreed.

"Every fisherman out here has his own theory." Ernest laughed. "But you científicos have to figure out who's right."

A half hour passed with nothing being sighted; then, finally, their luck changed. Juan, sitting on top of the cabin roof, was first to see it. Then as the wave broke everyone could make out a silver-purple bulk moving fast underwater, its wide pectoral fins spread like birds' wings. As it came out of the wave, you could see its purple stripes circling its long silver body. The swinging bill smacked the water by the left flat line. "Fish up, port line, fish up!" Juan called out in Spanish and then stomped his feet.

Carlos slowed the *Pilar* down and Ernest dropped back the line and took his seat again in the fighting chair. Mendez clipped the harness onto the rod as Ernest kept his thumb on the spinning spool. "Keep clear of the aft deck, gentlemen," Ernest commanded. "It can get a little hairy."

Cadwalader and Fowler grabbed the two wicker chairs and moved back, while Mendez and Samuelson cleared the other three lines. Papa then pressed hard on the wooden wedge to slow the speed of the spool of line.

"Oh she's a beauty," Ernest cheered as he locked the gear and jerked the rod back hard. He hit it again three times fast, setting the steel hook deep into the jawbone. Then Papa bucked forward in the fighting chair. He gave a yell and braced his feet for leverage against the heavy weight of the fish pulling on his arms; it was all he could do to keep himself from being yanked out of the chair. After the first several minutes with both arms straining, he felt the weight slack as the fish began to swim with the boat. The rod tip began to lift, then suddenly it bent double again and he watched the monster take the line out as quickly as it wanted. "Look at her," he commented. "This is the first run."

Another few minutes passed and Ernest lowered the rod and reel for the first time. It was a small victory, just a few feet of line. He gave another pull, and suddenly the line slacked as the great fish rose up out of the water, its twelve-foot-long body rising higher and higher until only the lower tip of the crescent tail touched the water's surface. Then, with the grace of a dancer, it moved across the waves, shaking its head and body. The spray gave off a brief, brilliant rainbow of red, blue and green.

"Herr Director," Ernest cheered. "You're buying dinner."

"My God—look at that fish—worth every penny." Cadwalader laughed.

"Hell, yes," Ernest managed between efforts.

"Just magnificent," Henry Fowler said, looking at the fish in mild shock.

"Don Carlos," Ernest barked to his mate, "better loop us around."

"*Sí*, Ernesto, " answered the old Cuban. The *Pilar* maneuvered in a circle ahead of the fish. Ernest continued to pump hard and reel, but the great fish kept taking out more line with each magnificent jump. Then it ran in short fits, greyhounding across the surface, stripping line and trying to shake or break the line. It all seemed more action than the crew could stand. In the first ten minutes, Ernest took in just over twenty feet of line and watched another two hundred run from the belly of the reel. In the end, it took all he had just to hold the rod tip up and watch it arc over in reverent homage to the great fish.

"Give him everything you've got," Cadwalader cheered. Ernest kept on pumping and reeling hard and fast. "Goddamn, what a fish," Hemingway growled, never taking his eyes from the line streaking across the water. He pulled back to pump the rod again and the marlin jumped three more times. Everyone on board was in awe at the way this giant rose up and hung in the air, its long, wet body blurring in great twists and bends, then crashing into a wave of white spray. The line sprang back like a banjo string and the beads of water fell from the line. The fish jumped again, this time hanging stiff and high in the air before falling.

Then the marlin tried to sound three times, and each time Papa held him and brought him back to the surface. By now both man and fish were tired, but the fish had it worse by far. It seemed confused, and made several tight circles while Ernest took in line quickly.

"You've got him," Mendez said.

"Agreed," Ernest said.

The marlin continued to swim behind the *Pilar*. "Now, Fowler," Ernest said with authority, "if you've been counting—this fish has been up over nineteen jumps—it can't go deep. Not with a gut full of air. He's tired, beat and floating on the surface."

Just then, the great marlin came back to life with a burst of energy. Line screamed off the reel, and the fish came up closer to the port side and flung himself in a somersault of splashing spray. "Look at him go!" yelled Cadwalader, his face bright as a child's. Then straight back from the *Pilar* the big fish surfaced again, floating higher and resting, flipping its fins slowly above with the waves. The marlin was only a dozen yards away—it was the moment of surrender and Ernest later captured it beautifully in his famous novella:

Then the fish came alive, with his death in him, and rose high out of the water showing all his great length and width and all his power and his beauty. He seemed to hang in the air above the old man in the skiff. Then he fell into the water with a crash that sent spray over the old man and over all of the skiff.

The big blue had nearly jumped itself to death. It floated a few yards off the stern, an easy target for sharks. "Carlos, get the rifle," Ernest commanded in Spanish.

"*Sí*," his first mate answered and disappeared into the cockpit below. A moment later, he reappeared holding Ernest's Mannlicher. Mendez took the gun and chambered a round.

"Are there sharks?" Cadwalader asked.

"Too early to tell," Ernest answered, taking in line. There was no sign of sharks, but Papa knew it was only a matter of time. The length of the fish was impressive; its black bill and huge body and strong tail rocked in the waves like a long blue log.

Papa glanced at his watch. "One hour, fifteen minutes. Don Carlos—the gaff, we've got a fish to get on board." But as the *Pilar* closed in the last few feet, the first shark appeared. He came straight up from the deep, mouth open.

"Shark, SHARK," screamed Cadwalader and Fowler. Carlos smacked at the water with the gaff and cursed as the black fin circled. The big blue raced across the surface with the shark in close pursuit.

"Murdering bastard," Ernest yelled. "Mendez, shoot it!" The sportsman took aim and fired the first of two shots just ahead of the moving fin. Then the water turned pink around the body of the shark, its white belly slowly rolling over and sinking under the water's surface.

"Good going," said Cadwalader.

"You got him," cheered Fowler.

Carlos backed the *Pilar* toward the marlin. As they closed the gap between the fish and the boat, Papa yelled, "Neutral, Carlos." The Cuban threw the gear into neutral and ran back to the transom. "Easy everyone, let Carlos through," said Papa and Mendez helped Ernest out of the fishing harness. Juan grabbed the leader with a gloved hand, and then all eyes were on Carlos as he braced himself and leaned out with the gaff toward the fish. In a single fluid motion, he dug the hook in and pulled the gaffed fish in close to the hull. Juan swung the wooden bat against the fish's head, ending its struggle.

Working together, the men lifted the great fish's head up as far as the roller, where Carlos slipped his knife through the soft tissue under the marlin's lower jaw and threaded a rope through the cut and out the mouth, where he tied it off to a pulley in the cabin.

"All right, men," began Ernest, "like the bloody Pharaoh said—give it a heave!" Everyone grabbed a hold of the rope and pulled. The great fish rose over the transom, and fell hard onto the deck between the two motor covers. Its long black bill reached just into the cabin door and its sickle-shaped tale brushed the transom.

"She's beautiful," said Cadwalader, taking in the rich blue hue that ran along the upper flank and shimmered against the belly of white-silver.

"She is a he," said Fowler as he began to examine the fish.

"Oh," nodded the director, "well, get on with it, Henry."

"Maestro, a round of drinks." Ernest grinned. "Highballs for everyone."

Fowler waved off his participation and instead pulled out his notebook. He began running a tape measure from tail to bill, and would end up taking a dozen measurements. After weighing in the marlin at the Casablanca docks, he would finish by cutting open the fish's stomach, examining the contents, figuring out its age and feeding patterns.

After a month of fishing every day, the científicos from the Philadelphia Academy of Natural History departed, armed with enough new information to revise the classification for marlin for the whole North Atlantic, and Ernest Hemingway had earned the title of naturalist. 🔲

Hemingway with members of the Philadelphia Academy of Natural History.

Hemingway's home in Key West, Florida.

LIFE AMONG THE CONCHS

CHAPTER № 06

By 1935, life was changing for Ernest Hemingway. The tourists had discovered Key West and the city fathers had listed the Hemingway house on the visitors' map, and needless to say Papa was not pleased. In the last two years, Pauline had completed all the renovation to their old, two-story Conch home, including replacing the ceiling fans with crystal chandeliers. But Ernest added icing to the cake when he hired a Key West newcomer, Toby Bruce, to build a six-foot-high fence around the entire property. The bricks for this wall had recently been removed from the city streets, to make room for the new prettier asphalt pavement.

Though the wall would give Papa back his privacy, Ernest yearned to leave Key West and head for the eastern side and deeper waters of the Gulf Stream. He had heard that Cuban politics were still murderous, so he decided that season to go to Bimini in the Bahamas.

Papa had heard that Bimini boasted the most iridescent blue-green water in the world, and an abundance of sea life riding in on the current of the Gulf Stream, which came within only a mile of the island's shore. Hemingway had read about fishing for giant tuna in Zane Grey's *Tales of Swordfish and Tuna*, an interest sparked by a glorious tuna sighting off Spain almost a decade earlier, when he and his first wife, Hadley, took their honeymoon voyage to Europe.

Hemingway aboard his boat, the Pilar.

In 1921, Ernest had written his father and family a letter describing what he saw off the ship's bow, a dozen six-foot-long, 300-plus-pound fish leaping clear out of the water. To Ernest, they looked more like horses jumping over fences, bursting with speed and grace. When the ship docked in Port Vigo, Spain, Ernest and Hadley found a fish market that had several of these giant fish gutted out on marble slabs, and he learned this species was called bluefin tuna.

Hemingway was captivated by the thought of landing one of these giants on rod and reel; he had dreamed of it for over a decade.

And yet, that first Bimini trip almost didn't happen. In fact, it could have cost Ernest his life. It began Sunday, April 7, 1935, a few hours after sunrise. Ernest was at the helm as the *Pilar* headed out to sea. On board were friends Mike Strater, John and Katy Dos Passos, and crew members Albert "Bread" Pinder, hired for his knowledge of engines and navigation, and another Key West Conch, Hamilton "Saca" Adams, who served as the *Pilar's* cook.

The plan for Bimini was for the crew to eat and sleep aboard. The *Pilar* could sleep seven with the dinette folded down into a double bunk and using the cockpit's bench bunks along with the forward double stateroom and the two mid-ship bunks.

Mike Strater, who was an artist friend of Ernest from his Paris days and the president of the Maine Tuna Club, suggested they troll the whole way across to Bimini. Ernest seemed in favor of a slow, easy trip. He had planned for a two-day crossing that would use the Gulf Stream's slow northerly movement to run up along Florida's coast, then anchor that night off Hawk's Cay. In the morning, he figured they would start the eastward leg to cross the Gulf Stream. The trip was a total of 232 miles from Key West to Bimini—well within the capabilities of the boat and its crew. The only thing they failed to bring aboard was luck.

The *Pilar* was only a few hours out of port, running twenty miles off the coast, when Ernest spotted a large green sea turtle swimming along a seaweed line. Instead of continuing on, Papa slowed his boat and circled back around, enticed by the prospect of turtle steaks, which was prized meat. In the time it took to come about, any sign of the hard-shelled creature had disappeared, but he spotted flashes of green and yellow under the brown seaweed. "What luck, gentlemen. Get the line out. We're into dolphin," meaning not the mammal but the wonderful eating fish.

A forty-pound bull dolphin hit the first line out. Strater took the rod and began to fight the fish. Dos Passos grabbed his new little movie camera and climbed up on the *Pilar's* cabin roof. "*El Presidente*," Ernest's nickname for Strater, "not too fast, got to let old Dos record the fight." Strater grinned and gave a wave to the camera. This was not a shy crew. In the cockpit, Katy Dos Passos stood next to Bread and Saca, watching the action.

Ernest gave the wheel to Bread, so he could have the next fish on. He took his shirt off and soaked it in a bucket filled with seawater. If he had learned anything about fishing, it was not to get overheated. He wrapped the wet shirt around his head like a turban and the damp cool felt good. "Hey, what do we call you now?" Dos Passos said with a laugh.

"How about Mahatma," Ernest said and picked up a rod and reel.

"What's that mean?" Katy asked.

"Old Master," Dos Passos said. "You don't have to get on his bad side to understand who's the captain or master of this vessel."

Ernest slacked the fishing line behind the stern. In a school of dolphin, it's only a matter of minutes before the next fish is on. Just then the port rod bent and Papa grabbed it. He had hooked a good size dolphin cow that jumped wildly. In the sun, the dolphin's bright green and yellow colors sparkled, and moments later the first shark appeared.

Dos Passos was the first to see it—a dark dot, coming up fast. The water exploded as the shark leaped and snapped Papa's fish in half. "Son-of-bitching shark!" Ernest cursed in Spanish and reeled the dolphin's head in.

"Better get your fish in," Ernest yelled.

But Strater's bull never had a chance. The shark took a mouthful of yellow and green. A moment later Ernest patted Strater on the back. "Congrats, Mr. President, you've hooked your first Florida shark."

"Pulls the same as the ones in Maine," Strater laughed and watched his rod bend double. He then began the task of pumping and reeling.

"Bring her back slow, Bread," Ernest told his helmsman. He gave a wave of his hand, while keeping his eyes focused on the spot where Strater's line entered the dark blue water. The *Pilar* came back into the lapping soft swells. The ocean was calm. It was a rare morning where the surface looks like an endless flat mirror, and rays of the morning sun turn the clouds a cheery pink. Suddenly, the mirror shattered as a dorsal fin broke through the surface. The shark was moving fast as its run pulled the belly of the reel's line out.

"Mucking *galano*," Ernest said, calling the shark by its Cuban name. "Don't give him any more line. Make the bastard work." Papa had a way of blending English and Spanish as a fight grew more passionate.

Strater kept pumping the rod and working the heavy fishing line in. He desperately wanted to impress Papa. On the next run, the shark broke clear of the water again, twisting and arching its back in a tangled mesh of wet-brown. Its wide fins splashed in the water and it began another run to pull out more line.

"What a wonderful sea-devil," Mike laughed. Ernest leaned over the transom with his rifle and fired a round. It hit the shark at the base of the dorsal fin. A cloud of red streaked behind in the wake. "Now he'll come willingly."

Strater watched as his fish made a new run. "Sure, Hem, just tell him that."

Following the trail of blood, a second shark surfaced.

"Shark up!" Dos cried from his rooftop perch. Ernest grabbed a rod and slacked line out to the second shark. It was a larger *galano*. Ernest had a striped bonito on the hook, and the new shark made two quick passes before charging the bait. The shark crashed it with such force that head and dorsal fin rocketed out of the water.

"All right, you SOB, let's see what you've got," Ernest growled, setting the hook. The big shark thrashed on the surface, kicking up foam. "Give me a fight, you illegitimate." He pulled hard on the heavy rod and watched as the fish jumped. Ernest turned to the helm. "Ease up the throttle, Bread. Let's tire this fish out." The engine whined as the gears slipped back into neutral. Strater kept working his shark, but it still had too much line out.

John and Katy Dos Passos aboard the Pilar in Bimini.

Katy looked up at her husband, filming from the *Pilar's* roof. "Are you getting this, John?"

"Oh yes, it's a fantastic view. Really quite wonderful," he said, punctuated by the rhythmic click of film turning inside the Bell and Howell movie camera.

"Dos, did you get the attack? The way that SOB flew out of the water?" Ernest asked.

"Yes, it was just beautiful."

Saca leaned in toward Katy and added, "That kind of beauty is why I don't swim."

"No matter how much we beg him," Ernest teased.

"No, not ever," the tan faced Conch added. "This old Stream would be my River Styx."

"What's all this talk of swimming, I got a fish on," the President laughed.

"Good," Dos cheered, "I'm running out of film. Get him to the boat."

But Strater's shark was on lighter tackle and still taking out line, while Papa steadily reined his fish into the boat. Finally Ernest called for the gaff. "Saca, get the hook."

But as Papa's fish came in, it suddenly spooked and with a splash of its tail, the big shark sank under a patch of floating brownish-yellow seaweed. Finally, a few minutes later, Papa brought the sharp-toothed monster alongside.

Strater's reel screamed again as his shark took off on yet another fast run. "Well, my friend," Ernest said, "I beat you to the leader."

"Indeed you did," Strater agreed.

"Well done, Old Master," Dos cheered from above.

Saca held the leader as Ernest took a quick swing with the gaff. He brought the hook up into the shark's throbbing gills. The steel set hard into flesh and the shark jerked and smacked against the wooden hull. Then, when it seemed to have settled down, Ernest and Saca lifted the six-foot shark head up to the roller. When its tail hit the side of the boat, it convulsed again and blood sprayed off in all directions. "You fornicating son of a bitch," Papa growled.

In a surge of adrenaline and testosterone, Hemingway pulled his Colt Woodsman .22-caliber pistol from his belt. He aimed for the sweet spot between the shark's eyes, intending for the bullet to hit the shark's brain and kill it instantly. But good plans sometimes go afoul and this one sure as hell did.

At the moment Ernest squeezed the trigger, the shark shook once more and cracked the wooden gaff. Missing its target, the bullet ricocheted off the brass stripping and shattered. Pieces of lead struck Ernest in both legs, and splinters from the gaff hit his right arm and face. The noise and commotion muffled the sound of the pistol shot, but Ernest knew what had happened.

"Well, I'll be a sorry son of a bitch," Papa said, glancing at the blood streaming down his legs. "I've been shot."

Katy stared in horror at the crimson wounds. "My God, your legs." She looked up to her husband; Dos Passos was already climbing down into the cockpit.

"How bad is it, Hem?" Dos asked, handing the movie camera to Katy. He bent down to take a closer look. A small deep hole three inches below the kneecap, another mushroom-shaped wound, and a half dozen more along the other calf were all spitting blood.

"Not so bad," Papa shrugged. "I don't feel any pain, or even discomfort." Strater and Dos Passos helped Ernest over to a wicker deck chair. "It's kind of a warm, sick feeling. Ohhh…my stomach."

Strater lifted Ernest's foot up and placed it on a crate. "Come on, Hem, aren't you going to tell us it's just a flesh wound?"

"But it's my goddamn flesh," Papa said and then retched with nausea. He lunged toward the deck bucket filled with seawater.

"You're going into shock, Hem?" Dos said. "Hell of a note. We better turn back."

Bread and Saca helped clean up the deck.

"What can we do for you, Papa?" Katy asked.

"Better get the iodine and hot water. Find out what kind of mess I've made."

Katy disappeared into the *Pilar's* cabin for a moment; Bread and Saca released the shark and watched it sink down into the dark, clear water. "Mike," Ernest yelled, "get that line in. We're going home."

Strater cut his line and stowed the rod. He came up under the cabin's shade roof and looked at Ernest's outstretched legs. "Sorry, Hem. I didn't hear any gunshot and thought you were kidding."

Bread turned back to Ernest, "Cap, you want a drink?"

"Not yet," Ernest answered. He took a deep breath and then let it out. "Jesus, the mucking shark gets me, and me in charge the whole time. Hell of a way to start a fishing trip."

"You always do like to make things lively," Dos joked and took a pan of boiled water from Katy. She passed over a towel and iodine. "You know," she scolded Ernest, "that could have hit any of us."

"Oh, Katy, you've known me since high school." He winced. "You know there would have been hell to pay...ahhh..." As Dos Passos wiped the blood from the deeper of the leg wounds, Ernest took a breath to continue. "...if I brought home no fish, no crew, and no guests either. Bread, better turn us back to Key West."

"Yes, Cap," Bread answered and goosed the throttle ahead. He spun the wheel slowly until the sports fisherman was turned around to the southeast, and then with the engines roaring, the *Pilar* pushed out of the water and came up on plane.

They made Key West before noon, and Ernest checked into the Marine Hospital and was given a tetanus shot. The doctor removed a dozen bird-shot-sized lead splinters, and all but one piece came out. But the one that eluded the reach of the tweezers was the largest and deepest. It remained ensconced in Ernest's left calf for the rest of his life. It did not, however, slow him down. After only six days of bed rest, Ernest was ready to try for Bimini again, but this time he did not fish along the way. With his wounds healing, he felt the best medicine would be the fresh air and sun.

Hemingway wrote about this accident in *Esquire* in June 1935, in a piece entitled, "On Being Shot Again: A Gulf Stream Letter": "On the way to Bimini we want to troll well out toward the axis of the Gulf Stream and see what we can raise. There is a lot of very fine looking current out there with a world of flying fishing in it, that we have had to cross going back and forth to Cuba and you cannot tell what we may hit. Your correspondent plans not to hit himself in the leg." ▨

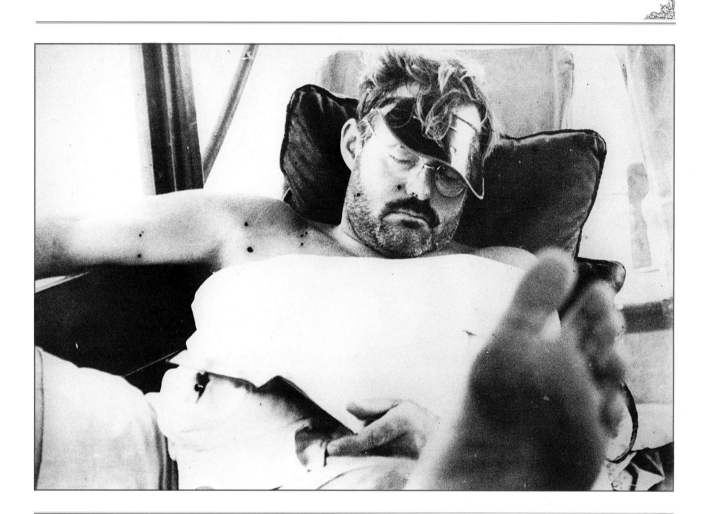

The Pilar, docked in Bimini.

BIMINI
THE OTHER ISLAND IN THE STREAM

CHAPTER № 07

O n April 14, twenty-six hours after leaving Key West, the *Pilar* and her crew docked in Bimini. Only Mike Strater stayed behind, replaced at the last minute by Ernest's Key West friend Charles Thompson. Strater rejoined the Bimini crew in May flying in from Miami on one of the daily Pan-American seaplane flights.

Ernest had just gone ashore when he met a broad shouldered, enthusiastic fisherman coming up the sandy road.

"Catch any?" asked Mike Lerner.

"No, going out first thing tomorrow."

"Great, I'll see you out there. By the way, I'm Mike Lerner," he said holding out his hand to shake with Ernest.

"Ernest Hemingway," Papa said shaking hands.

Hemingway and Lerner hit it off right away. After Lerner had made his millions on a women's clothing store chain, he devoted much of his life to sports fishing. He and his wife, Helen, with matching fishing boats, had made their home, The Anchorage, the unofficial embassy of the island. Lerner was in the process of building several smaller cottages on his property and after hearing about Ernest's work helping to identify the different marlin species, Lerner told Hemingway of his plan to establish an organization that would keep track of world record game fish caught. Lerner eventually founded the International Game Fish Association, and Hemingway held one of the founding vice-president positions until his death.

In Bimini, Ernest found a location to set his novel *Islands in the Stream*, and situated its hero Thomas Hudson in a home inspired by The Anchorage:

Hemingway and Mike Lerner celebrate their marlin catch.

Mike Lerner invited Hemingway to stay at his Bimini home, The Anchorage.

The house was built on the highest part of the narrow tongue of land between the harbor and the open sea. It had lasted through three hurricanes and it was built solid as a ship. It was shaded by tall coconut palms that were bent by the trade wind and on the ocean side you could walk out of the door and down the bluff across the white sand and into the Gulf Stream.

From his guest room at The Anchorage, Hemingway enjoyed views in all directions. Off to the east, moving through the flats, he saw flashes of silver he knew were schools of bonefish moving silently through the shallows. A lingering T-shaped shadow headed slowly out of the harbor to the south, one of the many oceangoing hammerhead sharks that circled the tiny island. He could see a sleek black manta ray moving parallel to the beach, its winged tips skimming the surface of the rolling surf. Despite the abundance of sea life around Bimini, what Hemingway wanted, what he hoped to catch did not come in close to shore. Due east of the island, well past the iridescent green and out into the dark oily blue of the Gulf Stream, sunlight reflected a sea of diamonds and the rolling swells contained fish he could only imagine.

View from Hemingway's guest room at The Anchorage. (Right) The Compleat Angler.

Charles Thompson, who had no luck hooking a marlin or tuna, left after a few days to return to his Key West hardware store. Ernest continued fishing and exploring the waters around Bimini. He, Bread and Saca slept aboard the *Pilar*, but Katy and John Dos Passos took one of the small bungalows on the island. John had a flare-up of his rheumatic fever while Katy began to suffer from severe stomach pains. The Dos Passos returned to Baltimore, where Katy quickly underwent surgery. She later told Ernest's wife Pauline that her "little operation" had been a D&C.

Ernest found Bimini a wonderfully isolated island filled with an odd assortment of sportsmen and locals, fine rum, swaying coconut palms and lovely water. The evenings were cool enough that he slept out under the stars on top of the *Pilar's* cabin roof, with just enough wind to keep the bugs off at night. Later, the evening rains drove Ernest to a room at Mrs. Duncombe's boardinghouse, The Compleat Angler. His letters home testified that the hotel had wonderful, clean rooms and good food.

Pauline flew to Cat Cay and then ferried to Bimini where she joined Ernest for a few days. She was impressed with the beauty of the island and felt it would be a wonderful place to bring the children later that summer. Pauline would first fly to St. Louis to pick up Ernest's oldest son, Bumby, who was arriving from Chicago, and then would return with Bumby, Patrick, Gregory and their nanny Ada Stern. She would not see Ernest until the end of June.

Alone in Bimini, Ernest wrote Jane Mason to come and visit him. Jane was one of the few women who Ernest felt understood him, his love for adventure, the sea, and his desire to conquer the monsters that lived in the Great Stream. But Jane cabled back that she could not join him, for at least several more weeks.

Ernest continued fishing with his two-man crew, but seemed much happier once John and Katy Dos Passos returned to Bimini. "Half the fun of fishing is spending time with your friends," he told Dos Passos over drinks at The Compleat Angler's bar.

"You know Kate and I would love to be out there with you Hem, but the doctors told Katy to take it easy." Dos said leaning over and taking another sip of his beer.

Pauline flew in on a seaplane to the island of Cat Cay, a short boat ride to Bimini.

Ernest raised an eyebrow.

"Give us a few days. I'll get her settled, we'll do some shelling, swimming, let me see how she does. Hem, you bring in the sea monsters, and we'll greet you at the dock."

Ernest understood, but did not stop missing his friends. He met often with Lerner and a half dozen other sports fishermen, most of whom were wealthy and enjoyed fishing all over the world. He wrote to his editor that he felt like the poor boy fishing among the rich, but that he had won $350 out-fishing them. Ernest was pleased to share with Lerner and others the Cuban fishing techniques that he had learned, including the use of multi-lines, and multi-depths for drift fishing, and the Cuban technique for rigging marlin baits. But Hemingway the teacher was also good at playing student, and was quick to notice that some of the fishing boats had developed topside helm controls, what would become the early forms of the flying bridge.

The *Pilar* had not come equipped with a flying bridge, but Ernest saw how others had fitted the cabin's roof with topside controls. Two years later Ernest rigged his in a similar fashion, though his early flying bridge was anything but fancy, consisting of an automobile steering wheel, pulleys and a steel bar superstructure. He wrote about the advantages this higher location gave him when marlin fishing:

Thomas Hudson swung down from the flying bridge into the cockpit and took the wheel and the controls there.... It was strange to be on the same level as the action after having looked down on it for so many hours, he thought. It was like moving down from a box seat onto the stage or to the ringside or close against the railing of the track.

ISLANDS IN THE STREAM

Ernest brought on board this trip to Bimini two new forty-four-ounce Hardy deep-sea rods, outfitted with Vom Hofe reels and Ashaway line. Ernest loved Russell's Hardy rods and had gotten used to the feel of the smooth roller guides and firm felt grips. He also had brought lighter rods and reels for his sons and guests to use.

Giant bluefin tuna boated off Bimini.

In his third week of fishing Bimini, Ernest finally got his chance to fight a giant tuna. Papa decided to head south of Bimini, instead of north, into a stretch of water between Gun Cay and Cat Cay that would later become known as *Tuna Fish Alley*. It was spectacular in the 1930s during the annual spring migration, and some considered it to be the best bluefin tuna fishing spot in the world, before commercial long-liners took their toll.

About an hour before sunset, when the sky filled with bright rays of orange and gold, the *Pilar* passed several skiffs and larger boats. All had gathered to watch an angler work a fish on a nearby sports fisherman. It was Bread who spotted the boat, as he scanned the sea with binoculars. "Hey, he's on to something big."

Ernest turned the ship's wheel and moved in closer. He squinted, looking out at the bobbing white hull.

"Isn't that's Cook's boat?" he asked.

"Looks like it," Bread agreed.

Ernest and his crew had met Charlie Cook, the manager of Cat Cay, a week earlier, sharing drinks and swapping fishing stories at Mike Lerner's home.

"Got to be a billfish. Look at the strain on the rod," Bread said.

"It's deep, whatever it is," Papa agreed. As they came in, Ernest made sure to give Cook a wide berth so he would have plenty of sea room. Ernest hated when spectator boats came in too close, often spooking the fish or cutting the fishing line. He could make out Cook planted in the fighting chair, his rod bent at a forty-five-degree angle, the line ready to pop at any moment. His body drenched in perspiration, his hands cut and bleeding, Cook was clearly into a fish that was too much for him.

"How's it going, captain?" Ernest yelled out.

"Tuna," Cook returned, "a thousand-pounder!"

"Honest?" Ernest shouted. He throttled back the *Pilar* with a little more respect. He did not want the blame for cutting the line on such a grand prize.

"Yeah. But the damn fish has won," Cook called out. "Six and half hours I've been fighting this son of a bitch. My hands are cut to shreds. I'm going to cut the miserable line."

"The hell you say!" Ernest yelled, "I'll take him. Not for the record, but to learn from him."

"Aww, crap, it's over, Hemingway," Cook said and waved him away.

"No," Ernest begged. "For the love of God, don't throw away a thousand-pounder!" Ernest was now leaning out over the cockpit, and Bread had the *Pilar's* helm.

"You really want it?" Cook asked.

"Absolutely—I'll come aboard."

"All right then," Cook agreed.

The *Pilar's* black hull slowly inched toward Cook's white sports fisherman.

"Saca, bring the Mannlicher up. I sure as hell don't want to lose this one to sharks," Ernest called. He kept his shark rifle on the forward bunk in a case lined with sheep's wool, and his affection for the weapon is apparent in *Islands in the Stream*:

It was a .256 Mannlicher Shoenauer with the old eighteen-inch barrel they weren't allowed to sell any more. The stock and forearm were browned like a walnut nutmeat with oil and rubbing, and the barrel, rubbed from months of carrying in a saddle bucket, was oil-slick, without a spot of rust.

ISLANDS IN THE STREAM

Saca handed Ernest the rifle. "Good luck, cap," the Conch said.

Ernest strapped the rifle over his shoulder and turned to Bread. "As soon I'm over, get her the hell out of here. In fact, go back and get Katy and John Dos Passos. They would want to see this marvel."

"Yes, cap," Bread agreed. The *Pilar* edged closer with each swell, the gap between the two boats becoming smaller, five feet, three feet, two feet. Ernest stood on the gunnel of the *Pilar* and then with the grace of a cat, jumped across into Cook's boat.

"Go—get Dos Passos and Katy, " Papa called and the *Pilar* lurched away. Bread waved from the helm and Saca gave the thumbs-up as the *Pilar* turned to run back to Bimini.

"Hemingway, welcome to my hell," Cook said, exhausted. Ernest looked at Cook's hands. His fingers were raw with blisters and the white gauze wrapped around his palms was soaked with blood. Cook had given this fish his all but it was not enough; his body had given out.

He could see David's bloody hands and lacquered-looking oozing feet and he saw the welts the harness had made across his back and the almost hopeless expression on his face as he turned his head at the last finish of a pull.

ISLANDS IN THE STREAM

"I've never seen a fish like this," Cook told Papa.

"Cool you down, Mr. Cook," a Bimini mate said and poured a bucket of sea water on Cook's back.

"Thanks, you boys take care of me all right."

"What were you fishing with? How did he hit?" Ernest asked.

"Eight pound bonito. Took the bait and sounded. The bastard stripped everything in under thirty minutes. I had fifty feet of line left when he slammed to a stop."

"Maybe he hit bottom," Ernest laughed.

"Maybe," Cook agreed and wiped at the perspiration on his forehead. "You sure you want this? I'm no closer now than when I started."

"Absolutely," Ernest said, pulling back on the rod slightly to relieve the pressure from Cook's grip. The Bimini mates quickly unbelted Cook from the fighting chair's harness. Ernest waited for the mates to lift Cook from the chair. His body was wet and limp. "Good luck, Hem," Cook said as he was carried to the cabin and collapsed on the bunk. The mates leaned over and lifted the sportsman's legs up onto the bunk and Cook closed his eyes at last.

Ernest settled into the fighting chair wet from Cook's sweat and clicked the harness tight. He pulled back on the heavy Hardy rod; the pole vibrated from the sheer weight and power of the fish. Papa couldn't be sure that the rod would stay in one piece, but if he were to get this fish in before the sharks showed up, he would have to trust the equipment. Slowly he began to pump and reel. Sometimes the line came in by the inch; sometimes he could get in several good cranks. The tuna had taken out 400 yards of line, and he was going to have to play this fish very carefully, or lose him in the deep.

Ernest knew to fight a fish after it sounded; the fish had to be pulled against the direction he wanted to go. The object was to wear him out and break his spirit, without forcing him to die deep. It took hours to raise a dead fish to the surface, and the sharks always found a way to the prize before the angler. Ernest began to form a new theory about the best way to boat one of these giant fish. He believed that if the angler could dominate the fight without letting up, he could convince the fish to give up. If done correctly, the fish would still have the speed to elude the sharks below, but not the will to fight the angler's line. This technique had worked for Ernest in Cuba on marlin and hopefully it would work here.

"Look," Ernest called to the white Bahamian running the boat, "when this fish sounds, run the boat in the direction of the line." He pointed off to the starboard. "See how the line slants in the water. We're not trying to tow the bastard. Just use the motor to shift our position. Play it like you're walking the saltwater flats with a bonefish. A very big goddamn bonefish." He looked at the heavy rod arcing out toward the stern. This fish was still very deep.

One of the Bimini mates offered Papa a cold Hatuey beer.

"Not till the fishing is over, thanks," Ernest said. True to his personal code, Hemingway rarely drank alcohol until the writing or fishing was done for the day. Illustrating this point, Ernest's son Patrick once said, "Dad once lost fifteen pounds from the sun's dehydration while fighting a big fish."

"Mister Hemingway," the taller of the two Bimini mates whispered, "your boat is coming back." Ernest looked to where the native pointed. There on the horizon was the *Pilar*, its black bow plowing through the rising blue seas. John and Katy Dos Passos were standing alongside Bread in the cockpit, waving. As they got closer, Ernest heard them shout, "How's it going, Hem?"

"Well, very well," Ernest returned, "Though we're losing the light."

"Can you see the fish?" Katy asked Bread as both looked off in the distance at a dark green-gray thundercloud rolling in from the ocean.

"No," Bread answered. "The fish is still plenty deep."

"Let's get on the roof, maybe we'll see better," Dos Passos said.

"No," Katy countered, looking at the rough weather. "I'd rather stay here on the deck." She was still weak from the surgery.

The two boats stayed within three hundred yards of each other as the last sliver of golden sun sank below the horizon. The pinks of the sky dimmed to blues, and filled up with an ocean of stars. Another hour passed and the thunderhead grew closer. A crack of thunder rattled the glass in the swaying cabin.

"I think we're in for some nasty weather," Bread said. "Better get below." Katy called out to her husband and within minutes the stars clouded over and the rain rushed to meet them.

Katy and John huddled together under a blanket in the open cabin. They watched the rain beat down the heavy seas, a soft veil covering jagged rocks. For a moment or two, the rain came down so hard that those on board the *Pilar* lost sight of Cook's boat completely. A few minutes later, a brilliant blue-white flashed through the sky, chased by a roar of thunder. "Aaaahhh!" Katy screamed. "Why is fishing with Hemingway always an adventure?"

Dos Passos laughed and gave his wife a hug. "It just is—just being with him is an adventure."

The smell of ozone filled the air and the sky lit up again as another strike moved between clouds. They saw Cook's boat and Ernest's profile in the fighting chair, rod doubled over. In the next flash, Bread pointed out some of the spectator yachts watching the fight were returning to shore. "Well," Katy laughed, "at least some folks know when it's time to get out of the rain."

On board Cook's boat, Ernest made steady gains, pumping and reeling fiercely. He had not rested since taking the rod. While the rain had been refreshing initially, it was now beginning to give him a chill. Cook sat just inside the cabin, and called out to Ernest. "You all right, Hem?"

"Fine, hope to hell the fish is enjoying this weather as much as I am."

"No doubt."

"Hey, Cook."

"Yes."

"You know whose boat that is, off the starboard?"

Cook looked out of the cabin. There, holding steady in the rough seas, was a lovely one-hundred-foot yacht. "Oh, that's the *Moana*," he answered. It was the only boat besides the *Pilar* that had not run from the storm. "It's owned by Bill Leeds, heir to the tin-plate fortune."

"I know Bill. Geez, that's some boat. He seemed a real stand-up guy."

"He is," Cook agreed.

As he looked over Leed's ship, the fishing line suddenly went slack. "I'll be a sonofa —" He began turning the crank handle on the reel.

"Aww, damn. Is he off?" Cook said, noting the rod straightening suddenly.

Just then Ernest felt the weight of the fish again. "No. He's coming up." A few minutes later, Cook saw it. "There! There it is!" he said, pointing out into the black waves.

Hemingway brandishes his new shark killer,
a Thompson submachine gun.

Cheers could be heard from the *Pilar*. Unexpectedly, a bright spotlight lit up the ocean and both boats, blinding all on board.

"Good grief," Katy growled, shielding her eyes. The light, they saw, was coming from Leeds's yacht. "Who does that man think he is?"

Leeds's captain tilted down the spotlight on the fish. The huge silver mass reflected through the wash of passing waves. It had been a hard three hours and twenty minutes of fight for Ernest and he was tired, but he showed no outward sign of exhaustion. "Oh, what a beauty. Fifteen yards and we've got him," Ernest said, reeling in the line. He was sure the tuna was world-record size.

"You did it," Cook whispered. "You really did it." Cook moved past Ernest to the transom of his boat. His eyes never left the large silver fish. Sharks had not touched it, not yet. Leeds's spotlight stayed on the giant tuna. Another horizontal sheet of rain moved across the water, soaking everyone through.

Ernest heard Dos shout his congratulations. Though the *Pilar* was keeping a respectful distance, all aboard could see the fish. Ernest heard several more admiring shouts from his crew and then from Leeds's yacht.

Ernest grinned and then looked back to his prize. But his joy and triumph dissipated as he saw one, three, five shark fins surface and begin moving in on the tuna. Like wolves they cut off any escape and hit with teeth bared. In the thrashing of blood and foam, the sharks ripped off twenty-five to thirty pounds of meat with each bite.

Over the melee, a new sound arose. "Rat, tat, tat, tat—rat, tat,

tat, tat!" Bill Leeds stood on the bow of his yacht, firing down at the streaking fins below, a Thompson submachine gun in hand. "Rat, tat, tat, tat—rat, tat, tat, tat!" The water exploded with red as two of the sharks rolled over, white bellies up. "My God," Ernest said, "that gun's got real shock power."

But there were too many of them, even with the Thompson. The sharks were feeding on their dead brothers as well as on the great tuna. Within minutes, the spotlight showed an ocean of red.

The tuna was finally brought alongside Cook's boat; all that remained was the head, backbone and tail. The sharks continued to hit what meat was left in the water. Angry, Ernest grabbed his rifle and fired three rounds into the feeding pack. He would later remember the intense disappointment of the moment:

He did not want to think of the mutilated under-side of the fish. He knew that each of the jerking bumps of the shark had been meat torn away and that the fish now made a trail for all sharks as wide as a highway through the sea.

THE OLD MAN AND THE SEA

Using block and tackle, the two Bimini mates hauled what was left aboard. The tuna's head would tip the scale at 249 pounds. After the marathon fish fight of nine hours and fifty minutes by two anglers, the crew finally secured the fish remains on deck. Cook returned to Cat Cay to recuperate, and Bill Leeds invited Ernest and the Dos Passos aboard the *Moana* for drinks while they dried out. They ended up spending the night in the yacht's comfortable cabins.

Leeds stayed up drinking with Papa. He seemed both amused and concerned about Ernest's anger over the sharks. "They are, after all, a part of fishing in Bimini," he told Ernest, "though this year, I'll grant you, is the worst I've ever seen." At some point that night, Ernest talked Leeds into giving him the famed Thompson submachine gun. John Dos Passos said later he was not sure exactly what deal was struck, only that by morning, Ernest was cradling his new shark-killer like a baby. Ernest would use the Thompson submachine gun on sharks for the rest of his big game fishing career, and praised the gun's precision in his writing:

He heard the submachine gun start firing from the stern and saw water start to spout all around the fin. Then it clattered again in a short burst and the water jumped in a tighter patch right at the base of the fin. ▨

ISLANDS IN THE STREAM

BOXING HEAVYWEIGHTS
PUBLISHER vs. WRITER

CHAPTER №̲ 08

One evening in May, Ernest found himself in an argument with a man he didn't know. Ernest had come in from a good day of fishing and though he had no big fish to show for it, he had hooked something big—probably a tuna that had played deep and given him a tough time before breaking the line. By the time his guests left, the *Pilar* was washed and the gear stowed; it was dark.

A voice down the dock called out to Ernest. "Say, aren't you the guy who claims he catches all the fish?"

Papa detected a large male figure standing in the shadows twenty yards off. Though he couldn't make out the face, he could see the man wore a nice shirt and pressed white shorts. "Say, aren't you the guy who claims he catches all the fish?" the man said again, and this time Ernest heard the slur in his voice. He didn't recognize the voice and couldn't imagine anyone he knew teasing him like this.

"I catch my share," Ernest answered.

"Where's the proof?" the drunk asked. "Or I suppose we're going to have to read all about some monster you almost brought in...or will you stand next to some fish you didn't catch and get your picture taken?"

"Look, I don't even know your name..."

"You slob. You filthy slob. Let's just find out if..." The man got louder as he saw several of the fishing captains coming onto the dock to see what all the yelling was about.

"If what?" Ernest demanded. "Maybe you need just one more drink. Why don't you just run along and get one?"

The Pilar at Bimini dock.

"Oh no. You lousy writer, I want satisfaction, or I'll shame you off this dock. Are you yellow, Hemingway?" The man set himself into a crouching boxing stance. "Show me what you got, you big fat slob." Several more fishing captains, including Howard Lance, Bill Fagan and Ernest's friend Ben Finney, along with a dozen locals, stepped onto the dock. The man, surrounded by the crowd, seemed to gain courage. Ernest tried one last time to talk him out of it.

"You don't know what you're getting into. You're just talking big so you can repeat what you've said to your New York friends and that's horseshit!"

"Trying to get out of it, that's just what I figured."

Ernest was up on the dock in three barefoot leaps. His heckler lunged at him as he came up. Ernest clipped him three times with left hooks, but the drunk didn't go down. Instead he charged Papa like a football linebacker, and Ernest felt himself being pushed toward the water. This was one fight he did not want to continue in the water. Ernest punched the drunk twice hard on the side of the head, backing him up just enough for Papa to land a solid Sunday punch. The drunk flung his head back and was out cold before his massive body crumpled to the dock.

"You know who that is?" Captain Bill Fagan asked Ernest.

"Nope," Papa answered, wiping his brow. He glanced up to see people gathered around them on the dock.

Ernest considered boxing an excellent form of exercise, and enjoyed instructing Bimini locals.

"Joseph Knapp," Captain Fagan said. "Owner and publisher of *Collier's*, *McCall's* and *American* magazine."

"No kidding... well, that's what I call limiting your magazine markets." Ernest wiped the blood off his knuckles and left the dock to wash up at The Compleat Angler.

Members of the Bimini calypso band later celebrated Ernest's victory with a song, "Big Fat Slob." Under the swaying palm trees around the garden of the Compleat Angler, Nattie Saunders's sweet voice rose above the tinny melody of the metal drums: "This the night we have fun. Oh, the Big Fat Slob in Bimini. This the night we got fun. Mr. Knapp called Mr. Ernest Hemingway a Big Fat Slob. Mr. Ernest Hemingway balled his fist, and gave him a knob. Big Fat Slob in Bimini, this the night we have fun." Everyone danced and drank and turned a minor brawl into an island legend.

In spite of the wisecracks, Leicester Hemingway said that Ernest grew worried that he might have seriously hurt his opponent. Around four in the morning Knapp's yacht, *Storm King*, left Bimini for Miami because the captain wanted to get medical attention for his boss. Despite the trouble, Knapp later was fair about the whole incident. He told Captain Fagan to tell Ernest he was sorry, that he had spoken out of turn and guessed he had gotten what he deserved. Ernest later recaptured the moment in *Islands in the Stream*:

"You slob," the man said across the space of water that separated the two boats the same way someone might speak insultingly to an animal in one of those modern zoos where no bars, but only pits, separate the visitors from the beasts. "You phony."....

"Look," Roger said to him. "You're not talking to me at all. You're just talking to be able to repeat back in New York what you said to me."

He spoke reasonably and patiently as though he really wanted the man to understand and shut up.

"You slob," the man shouted, working himself further and further into this hysteria he had even dressed up for. "You rotten filthy phony."....

Roger stepped quickly over to where the man stood and raised his left shoulder and dropped his right fist down and swung it up so it smashed against the side of the man's head.

ISLANDS IN THE STREAM

Despite his assertion, Hemingway had not limited his magazine market by any means. In fact, it would be through *Collier's* magazine that Ernest would help a young writer named Martha Gellhorn.

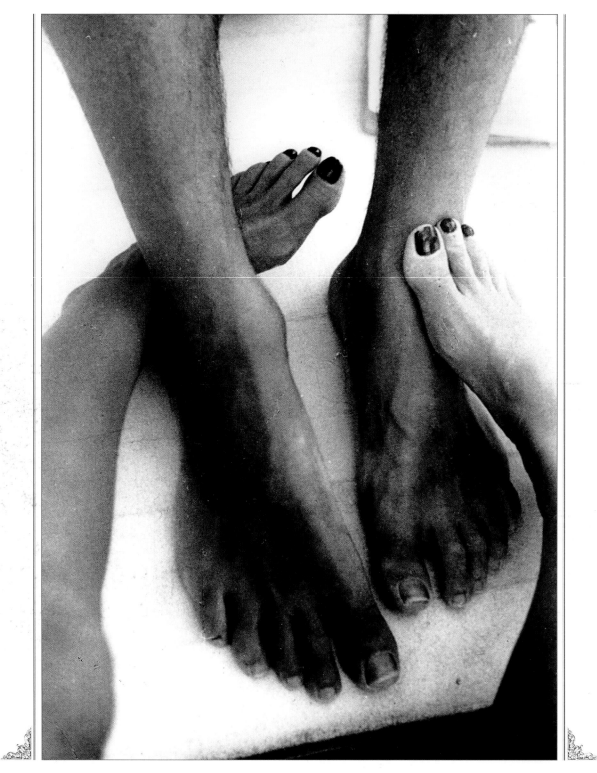

Ernest and Martha share a tender moment.

MARTHA GELLHORN
WIFE OR WAR CORRESPONDENT

CHAPTER № 09

In 1936, Hemingway walked into Sloppy Joe's, Josie Russell's bar, just off Greene Street. A lovely young woman in a black dress, with blond hair and long legs, sat at the bar.

She sat on a high stool with her legs tucked under her and looked out at the street. Freddy looked at her admiringly. He thought she was the prettiest stranger in Key West that winter. Prettier even than the famous beautiful Mrs. Bradley.

TO HAVE AND HAVE NOT

The stranger was Martha Gellhorn and Mrs. Bradley, Jane Mason. Hemingway introduced himself and ended up buying a round of drinks for Martha Gellhorn, her mother Edna, and brother Alfred, and as it turned out they had just arrived on the island. The midday tourists from St. Louis stood out at Sloppy Joe's Bar, which was better known for its clientele of charter boat captains and seedy sailor types. Ernest invited the Gellhorn family for a tour around town in his car, playing the part of the tourist guides he so detested.

Ernest learned that Martha, a writer, already had two novels published. She had just recently returned from researching her third book in Germany, and spoke at great length of her concern with the rise of the Nazi party. Martha decided to stay on a couple weeks after her mother and brother left. Already an admirer of Hemingway, she wanted to get to know him better. Pauline didn't seem too bothered by her company; Ernest had been attracted to other women in the past.

According to Les Hemingway, the affair between Martha Gellhorn and Ernest Hemingway began in Key West, but became more serious when Martha followed Ernest to Spain. Martha Gellhorn said that she had come to Madrid and "tagged along behind the war correspondents, experienced men who had serious work to do."

Martha Gellhorn.

She had not intended to join their ranks, but when she arrived in Spain, Martha had in her possession a letter from *Collier's* magazine stating, "To whom it might concern, that the bearer, Martha Gellhorn, is a special correspondent from *Collier's* in Spain." The letter was a gift from

Kyle Crichton, the editor of the magazine, intended to help her smooth over situations with any authorities wondering what a nice girl was doing in the war-torn city. In truth, Hemingway had arranged the whole thing. It meant nothing; Martha did not yet have an official connection with a magazine or a newspaper.

She met up with Ernest at the basement restaurant of the Gran Via Hotel.

"Ah Marty, you made it, I knew you would."

"That's funny, I wasn't so sure myself," she said. She kissed him and took a seat at the table with Hemingway and the other fellow correspondents.

"What we have to do now is write," Ernest said to the group. "As long as there is a war you always think perhaps you will be killed—so you have nothing to worry about. But we are not dead, so we must write." He took another shot of whisky, and added, "Living is much harder than dying and damn if writing isn't harder than living."

Martha looked around the room, filled with foreign war correspondents. Most seemed a bit drunk, a few just stared at her golden hair as if she were an angel who had come for them. She reached into her knapsack and pulled out some money for a drink and a room, but Papa interceded.

As the days went on, and the group left the city to report on the war, she began to feel better about her decision to come to Spain to be with Ernest. Martha wrote about being in Spain: "I believed that all one did about a war was go to it, as a gesture of solidarity, and get killed, or survive if lucky until the war was over.... I had no idea you could be what I became, an unscathed tourist of wars."

Martha was spending her time learning Spanish, and visiting the wounded. Ernest suggested that if she wanted to better serve the cause, she should write about the war. To give her a better view of the battlefields, he took her on a ten-day tour on horseback through the mountains. He suggested that she write about Madrid, about the people's daily life amid the strife of war. Although Martha had never before reported on a war, she took his encouragement and wrote her first piece. She submitted it to *Collier's* with little expectation, and was surprised when *Collier's* published the piece, and added her name to its masthead: "I learned this by accident. Once on the masthead, I was evidently a war correspondent. It began like that."

By the war's end, Ernest had come to realize another great truth. In a letter to his editor he wrote, "We know war is bad. Yet sometimes it is necessary to fight. But still war is bad and any man who says it is not is a liar.... The only thing about war once it has started, is to win it—and that is what we did not do. The hell with war for a while, I want to write."

Leaving Key West and a broken marriage behind in 1939, Ernest returned to Cuba and began work on a new book about the Spanish Civil War.

In April of that year, Martha joined Ernest in Havana and took up residence at the Ambos Mundos. But while the hotel was a fine place for a short visit, Martha wanted a more permanent home and took it upon herself to find a house to rent.

The Finca Vigía, Hemingway's home in Cuba for twenty years.

Downstairs at the Ambos Mundos bar she found Ernest sipping on a beer. "Look here, it has a pool, tennis court, and acres of mango trees," Martha said, waving the classified section of the newspaper.

Ernest's face brightened. "Let's go see it, daughter."

As the car rambled past the banana and coconut tree farms along the way, Ernest seemed bothered by the distance they were covering. "You know Marty, this is quite the drive."

"Yes, but it's quiet and the air is fresh."

They passed some schoolchildren walking along the road. Ernest slowed down and waved at the group. In Spanish he asked directions and the young boy smiled and pointed wildly ahead. As they drove off, Martha giggled and said, "Well, at least they're friendly out here."

Owned by the D'Orn family, the Finca Vigía, meaning "Lookout Farm," had fallen into disrepair. A friend of the family met them at the gate and unlocked it. As their car dove up the tree-lined driveway, Martha fell in love with the place immediately. Ernest liked the shade trees, but his enthusiasm dropped when the car pulled around the circular driveway to the front of the house. The walls, once white, were peeling and stained with black mold. Ernest was unimpressed, though Martha regarded the Finca as a diamond in the rough.

"You can't be serious," Ernest said walking through the empty old house. "They want a hundred a month for this place. Look at it, for Christ's sake."

Martha aboard the Pilar; at Finca Vigía.

"I am. And I am falling in love with it," Martha said looking dreamy-eyed as they walked down a tree-lined path to a large pool filled with green algae and broken branches. Ernest turned, and took Martha in his arms. "What are you talking me into—I really think this place needs a lot of work."

"I don't," she said.

"It's so far from Havana—from the Stream."

"It's perfect. Trust me," she said and gave him a kiss.

"You'll have to do better than that," he said and kissed her again with passion.

Ernest and Martha returned to the Ambos Mundos, where Ernest continued his work on *For Whom the Bell Tolls*, a novel he would eventually dedicate to her. The heroine Maria shared many of Martha's physical characteristics, such as having blond hair that flowed "like a wheatfield in the wind," though the story opens with her hair growing back after being shaved:

"Qué va," Robert Jordan said and reaching over, he ran his hand over the top of her head. He had been wanting to do that all day and now he did it, he could feel his throat swelling. She moved her head under his hand and smiled up at him and he felt the thick but silky roughness of the cropped head rippling between his fingers. Then his hand was on her neck and then he dropped it.

"Do it again," she said. "I wanted you to do that all day."

FOR WHOM THE BELL TOLLS

While Ernest was on a fishing trip, Martha took the time to oversee a small crew of painters, plumbers, electricians, gardeners and maids hired to fix up the house. Within a few weeks, Ernest returned to the Finca and was so delighted with the improvements that they moved in promptly. He was quick to write his editor to tell him about the Finca and what he hoped would be his future with Martha.

Dear Max: ....It is fine out here in the country. There are quit[e] a lot of quail on the place and lots of doves. Patrick and Gregory were over for [t]he holidays and they had a fine time. I wish you could see this joint. Hope can renew the lease in June.

I don't care about going to war now. Would like to live a while and have fun after this book and write some stories. Also like the kids very much and we have good fun together. Also would like to have a daughter. I guess that sounds funny to man with five of them but I would like to have one very much.

Martha, however, did not seem overly anxious to have children. She had lived with Ernest for three years before Ernest's divorce from Pauline was finalized. By the end of November, she and Ernest were married, and shortly after Ernest heard a friend ask Martha after the wedding if she planned to now write under the name Martha Hemingway. He was surprised by her answer: "Absolutely not."

Ernest made a Christmas gift to Martha and to himself, using the money from the successful *For Whom the Bell Tolls* to purchase the estate for 18,500 Cuban pesos. But the honeymoon in their new home was short-lived. *Collier's* magazine sent a cablegram agreeing to Martha's request to send her to cover the war in China.

"Great, my wife's idea of a honeymoon is to stroll down the Burma Road," Hemingway joked to Ralph Ingersoll, the publisher of *PM* magazine.

"Why don't you join her," Ingersoll suggested. "You can write for us, Hem."

Ernest took Ingersoll up on the invitation and both Ernest and Martha left shortly after for China. They stayed their first month in Hong Kong, and Ernest wrote his family that "morale was high and morals were low." The fact that the British Crown Colony was crawling with beautiful young prostitutes made Martha eager to leave for the 7th War Zone HQ in Shaokwan.

Though she did not complain at first about the cold or the stink of war, she was appalled when their hotel put up a sign up asking guests not to kill any bugs on the walls, as it would ruin the wallpaper.

"Ernest," she begged, "you've got to get me out of this country."

But they did not leave and instead both went on to cover more of the war, traveling through the battle-torn country and meeting with villagers, soldiers and commanders alike. Then in the 103-degree heat under the golden spires of a temple in the Rangoon jungle, the newlywed couple had their first big falling out. Ernest decided it was time to return to Hong Kong, get his articles written and go home. But Martha wanted to follow a story lead that would take her on into Jakarta. It seemed clear to Ernest that Martha's professional ambition as a war correspondent was more important to her than wifely responsibilities, so Ernest left Hong Kong and waited for Martha to join him in New York. When she finally did arrive, they headed south together, stopping once in Washington and then in Key West, where he learned of Joe Russell's death.

Ernest wanted to settle down at the Finca again and write. He had seen enough death, both of strangers and friends. He envisioned himself and his wife writing fine novels and starting a family together, and Martha seemed content at first with the plan. She had built good relationships with Ernest's sons, Jack, Patrick and Gregory. When they weren't out fishing with their father, they would join Martha for swims in the pool or games of tennis.

One day, several local San Francisco de Paula boys came

Gregory and Patrick were quite fond of Martha.

over the fence to pick the ripening mangos. The previous owner had kept large dogs and the boys had not dared to enter, but now they were quick to toss rocks up into the trees, trying to knock down the brightest of the yellow-orange fruit. Ernest saw the boys and came quickly down the pathway.

Gregory Hemingway (left) with two Gigi-All-Stars teammates; neighborhood boys playing baseball on the grounds of Finca Vigía.

"Hey, knock it off," he yelled in Spanish. "Leave the bloody trees alone. You can have the fruit—but don't harm the trees."

Just then, an older black Cuban boy, Oscar Blasquez, let a rock fly that hit its mark, the largest ripest mango, seventy feet into the trees.

"Damn, you've got some arm, kid," Ernest said. Then, holding up his hand to stop anyone else from throwing rocks, he added, "You boys should have your own baseball team!"

That got their attention. Ernest then introduced his son Gregory to the local kids, and by the following day they had organized into a team with brand-new gloves, balls and bats. The team Papa called the Gigi-All-Stars, named after his son Gregory. By summer's end they had played most of the kids from neighboring towns. The summers, as Ernest saw it, were for his family.

Even Bumby came over from Paris and joined his father and brothers. Ernest's desire for a solid family played heavily into the psyche of the character Thomas Hudson:

He had always loved his children but he had never before realized how much he loved them and how bad it was that he did not live with them. He wished that he had them always and that he was married to Tom's mother.

ISLANDS IN THE STREAM

Hemingway at work at Finca Vigía.

In an effort to establish a normal family life in Havana, Ernest had hired a cook, a maid, a gardener, and a chauffeur to help around the Finca. He liked it best when the house was filled with the cheerful sounds of kids at play, and when the summer ended and the boys left, Hemingway always felt desperately alone. The Finca's only curse and reward was its solitude. Work was how Papa handled his loneliness, and he found in the cool of the morning, it was possible for him to remember all the places he had been before, the things he had seen, and people who had stories worth telling:

All he cared about now was that the boys were coming over and that they should have a good summer. Then he would go back to work.

He had been able to replace almost everything except the children with work and the steady normal working life he had built on the island…. Now when he was lonesome for Paris he would remember Paris instead of going there.

In 1942, young Gregory won a gold medal for his eagle-eye marksmanship. The metal was engraved, "To Gigi as a token of admiration from his fellow shooters, Club de Cazadores del Cerro." Ernest took great pleasure telling of his sons' accomplishments to friends. He had as guests two exiled Basques who had fought for the Loyalists and were now supporting themselves by playing professional pelota at the Havana jai alai fronton. "Imagine Gigi," he began in Spanish to Paxtchi and Dine, "At nine, Gigi has beaten out two dozen of Cuba's finest shooters." Ernest laughed. "I tell you—if we ever get overrun by the damn Nazis, my boys and I will hold them off just fine."

The threat of Nazis along the Cuban coastline had become very real. A number of cargo freighters and Allied ships had been sunk along Florida's coast, and up to five German U-boats spotted off various ports along the Caribbean.

Ernest even introduced his kid brother, Leicester, to Englishman Tony Jenkinson, a correspondent for the *London Daily Express* who had an immediate assignment from British Naval Intelligence. Jenkinson came to Ernest asking if he knew someone who could sail and wanted to do some exciting work. "Sure I do," Ernest said, "the best sailor in our family, my kid brother, Les." Of course, Leicester was the only family member who had any real experience on sailboats, having built his own eighteen-foot sloop and sailed it across the Gulf of Mexico from Mobile to Key West without an engine or paddle. While understanding sailing did not really qualify Les as a submarine hunter, it was the best Papa could offer.

Three months later, Les and Jenkinson returned to Havana with photographic evidence of German U-boat refueling stations. While the British were happy with the findings, Washington's brass did not accept them. Ernest decided to take matters into his own hands and devise his own operation, one over which he would exert full control. 🕸

Hemingway's dog Narita (left) and cat Boise (right) appear in Islands in the Stream.

Hemingway and crew aboard the Pilar, headed out into the Gulf Stream.

THE CROOK FACTORY

CHAPTER № 10

Determined to put his plan into action, Ernest first approached Ellis Briggs and Bob Joyce at the American embassy. After he detailed his plan to assemble a private counterintelligence group of his Cuban contacts to monitor the German spy activity in Havana, Briggs and Joyce arranged for Hemingway to meet with the American ambassador, Spruille Braden. Ernest left the meeting with the ambassador's cautious approval to proceed with his plan, as well as the use of a Radio Direction Finder (RDF) and other government equipment. What was initially called Operation Friendless became the Crime Shop and finally, the Crook Factory. Accordingly, Hemingway's vision shifted. No longer content with tracking German spies or local sympathizers, or even documenting submarine refueling sites, he set his sights higher: capturing a German U-boat.

Hemingway with his beloved cat Boise.

He had heard reports of turtle fishermen along the north coast of Cuba who had encountered German subs. One had barely made it back alive after a U-boat surfaced while he was fishing close to the Cay Sal Bank. Huge air bubbles rising to the surface, the great black and gray hull of the Seawolf submarine had emerged from the water. The fisherman had raised his sail quickly, but thoughts of outrunning the U-boat had been arrested by the sound of gunfire coming from the deck. The fisherman had no choice but to be boarded. The Germans took his catch and every bit of food and fresh water he had on board.

As Ernest mulled over the story, inspiration struck: If he could lure a German sub to the surface to take his catch, he could attack. Clearly, destroying the sub was out of the question, but it would not be necessary—merely disabling it and preventing it from submerging would be enough. The Germans would be forced to run on the surface, and they could be tracked until their fuel ran out. It was a plan, he thought, pouring a fresh drink, a very good plan.

A black and white cat walked into the room and jumped up on Papa's lap. He purred as Hemingway ran his hand down his spine and flank. "Boise, have you been out hunting?" Ernest held the cat in his arms and listened to the loud purring. Boise leaned forward and rubbed his chin against the lip of Hemingway's glass. "Hell yes," Ernest finished. "We're going to lure the Kraut bastards up—then, like you—we'll pounce."

When he woke he listened to the noises of the night birds and he was awake and listening when he heard Boise leap up onto the window ledge. Boise was a very silent cat. But he called to the man as soon as he was on the window ledge and Thomas Hudson went to the screen and opened it. Boise leaped in. He had two fruit rats in his mouth.

ISLANDS IN THE STREAM

At sunrise, Ernest drove to the town of Cojimar to meet with Captain Gregorio Fuentes, the first mate of the *Pilar.* Ernest hired Fuentes in 1938 after Jane Mason had hired away Carlos Gutierrez to run her boat, an action that Ernest perceived as retaliation for his falling in love with Martha Gellhorn. As the new mate, Captain Fuentes had proved his worth right away, keeping the *Pilar* the cleanest ship Ernest had ever seen. After several years of this maintenance, Papa knew Fuentes preferred the work of keeping a ship clean, painted and varnished to fishing. He also knew that the man would rather fish than eat or sleep.

The fortified tower at Cojimar.

Driving the road bordering the Cojimar harbor basin, Ernest passed the fortified tower at the mouth of the harbor, built in 1649 by the Spanish to protect Havana against pirate raids. The Cubans had used the tower for years as a lookout post, and the fishing village that grew up around the harbor and fort had come into its own only in 1907, when the first pier was built out from a seawall that protected the deep side of the harbor.

Papa kept the *Pilar* anchored just off the pier, and had it swing on the anchor instead of rubbing against the old dock. Captain Fuentes lived in a small house two blocks from the harbor basin, and kept a rowboat tied to the dock that he used to go out to the *Pilar.* Not a day passed that Fuentes did not look after her. He was already headed down to check on the boat when Hemingway's Lincoln turned the corner at his house.

Fishing boats at Cojimar.

Fuentes smiled and crossed the street to get into the car. "Are we fishing today, Papa?" Fuentes asked.

"No," Hemingway said. "Today we're looking for another kind of catch. We're going fishing for information."

As they began a long trip through the countryside, heading for the fishing town of Romano Archipelago in northwest Cuba, Ernest spoke to Fuentes about the German submarines. As many as thirty-five Allied ships a week were being sunk in the Gulf of Mexico, the Florida straits, and the Cuban and Bahamian waters. Both men had heard about the fishermen who had encountered the U-boat crews; now it was time to meet them.

Sitting at a café by the water, Hemingway and Fuentes met with the turtle hunters and listened to their firsthand accounts of encountering the German submarines. They had seen two merchant ships, a freighter named the *Olga* and a tanker called the *Texan*, sunk off the coast at night. Hit by torpedoes, the ships had gone down in fiery explosions. This was not rumor, sprung from the imagination of fishermen, but the first concrete proof of a sea wolf sub prowling the area.

Fishermen in a vivero.

Papa asked the fishermen to describe in detail the behavior of the submarine crews when they surfaced and demanded the fishermen's catch. It was crucial to establish if there were set procedures of boarding the *viveros*, or fishing boats; he wanted to get inside the head of the German commander. As they interviewed each fisherman about their encounters, Hemingway paid special attention to details of the size of the sub and the height of the conning tower. If the tower stood too tall from the water's surface, Papa's plan would not work. He also wanted to know the width of the hatch, and if the fishermen could see if they left it open when they boarded the turtle boats.

Only one of the fishermen had gotten a good look at the submarine in the bright noon sun. After being forced to turn over his catch, he was surprised to see the crew go ashore to a neighboring island. Clearly, they were searching for more food and portable water, and the island's *tortugueros*, turtle hunters, tried to stop them from stealing the bananas and vegetables in their gardens, without success.

"If they are that hungry," Ernest said to Fuentes, "damnit, we will place our catch out in plain view. When they call us alongside, the boys will clear the deck with the machine guns and Paxtchi will throw the bomb into the hatch."

"But what about their weapons, Papa?" asked Fuentes as they rode home in the Lincoln.

"If we're alongside, we're out of the way of the torpedoes. The bomb will either blow the watertight hatch, or fall below and explode in the periscope control area. Either way, the sub won't get away."

By the time Hemingway and Fuentes returned to the Finca, Ernest had composed a checklist for the mission. The German attack subs were known to make twenty knots on the surface, nearly twice the speed of the *Pilar*'s seventy-five horsepower Chrysler, so he decided to have the *Pilar* overhauled at the Casablanca shipyards. Hemingway ordered certain modifications for the *Pilar* to make her combat ready, including two new larger gas motors and four sheets of steel plating to be fitted on both port and starboard sides of the hull.

"Good Lord, Hemingway, what are you doing to your vessel?" asked Winston Guest, a millionaire sportsman, standing with Ernest and Fuentes in the shade of a white schooner up on the ways. The men watched as workers draped the *Pilar*'s black hull with rusty sheets of steel.

"Wolfie, thank you for coming. With this armor, the *Pilar* will be able to take a direct hit from the Krauts' five-inch deck gun." Ernest clapped his hand on Guest's shoulder. "I am also thinking of adding two fifty-caliber machine guns."

"Fifty-caliber? Where in bloody hell will you find those?" Guest asked.

"I have a fine assortment of friends," Hemingway said.

That night at the Finca, the Crook Factory held its first meeting. In attendance were Winston Guest; John Saxon, a radioman on loan from the American embassy; Basque Merchant Marine Juan Dunabeitía, a.k.a "Sinsky," or "Sinbad the Sailor"; a Barcelona bartender named Fernando Mesa; Francisco "Paxtchi" Ibarlucia, a Basque jai-alai player; a second Basque player known only as Dine; Don Andres Untzain, a Spanish priest; and Captain Gregorio Fuentes. Including Hemingway, the crew numbered nine members.

Hemingway and crew leaving Havana harbor.

The Crook Factory held meetings at all hours of day and night, laying out their mission strategy and talking over how and where to acquire weapons. The American Embassy finally supplied some very expensive radio equipment, but only after Hemingway had signed and vouched for it personally.

It was the last thing to be loaded on the ship before it left the shipyard on what would turn out to be the shortest voyage the *Pilar* ever attempted. Before the *Pilar* even made its turn for Cojimar, the crests of passing waves were coming dangerously close to washing over the bow. The weight of the steel sheets pushed the bow into the waves; she looked as though she were about to become her own U-boat. Ernest almost laughed when he saw the look of concern on Fuentes's face.

"This is not right," the Cuban said.

"Agreed, but what will happen once we get up on plane?" Ernest asked and took over the helm, pushing the throttles open on the two new engines. But while the motors whined higher, the bow failed to rise up on plane. In fact, the boat's speed did not seem to change at all.

"Ah shit," Ernest growled. He spun the ship's wheel and the *Pilar* headed back toward the shipyard. "We're as graceful as a pregnant pig."

While it had taken days to fashion the armor plates and affix them to the hull, they came off in a matter of hours. Shortly after, Hemingway and his Crook Factory crew began daily patrols along the Cuban coastline, sometimes going so far to the northwest that they would stop overnight in the deep lagoons along the mangrove islands. Much of the Crook Factory's sea hunt served as the basis for Thomas Hudson's chase of Nazi sailors:

They came in toward the line of green keys that showed like black hedges sticking up from the water and then acquired shape and greenness and finally sandy beaches. Thomas Hudson came in with reluctance from the open channel, the promising sea, and the beauty of the morning on deep water, to the business of searching the inner keys.

ISLANDS IN THE STREAM

Ernest hung signs on the port and starboard of the *Pilar* reading, "American Museum of Natural History." Their goal was to lure a submarine to the surface to demand the *Pilar*'s catch, and that meant the *Pilar* had to be seen fishing. Ernest made sure the men of his Crook Factory dressed and acted the parts of the scientists from the Museum. Much like Thomas Hudson, Hemingway had his men dress the part:

When they were scientists no weapons showed and they wore machetes and wide straw hats such as Bahaman spongers wear. These the crew referred to as "sombreros científicos." The larger they were the more scientific they were considered.

"Someone has stolen my scientific hat," a heavy-shouldered Basque with thick eyebrows that came together over his nose said. "Give me a bag of frags for science's sake."

"Take my scientific hat," another Basque said. "It's twice as scientific as yours."

"What a scientific hat," the widest of the Basques said. "I feel like Einstein in this one. Thomas, can we take specimens?"

"No," the man said. "Antonio knows what I want him to do. You keep your damned scientific eyes open."

ISLANDS IN THE STREAM

While keeping their eyes open, the Crook Factory listened. Hemingway had installed the RDF equipment, knowing he would owe the U. S. Navy $32,000 if it incurred any damage. But with it on board, Hemingway knew he could follow the communications of the German submarines and get a fix on their positions. The RDF took up most of the forward cabin, and Hemingway set it up with a chart table in order to plot position and course. Now Ernest and the crew felt they could take the initiative in the sub hunt, instead of waiting for one to come their way.

Hemingway displayed this picture of the Pilar on a bookshelf at Finca Vigía, where it remains today.

OF SHARKS AND SUBS

CHAPTER № 11

In his memoir, *Misadventures of a Fly Fisherman*, Jack "Bumby" Hemingway gives his firsthand account of life on Papa's sub patrol: "Papa invited me to come on one of the 'combat' patrols of the Pilar along with Winston Guest, who was now called Wolfie, and the rest of the crew. There was no sighting of any U-boats. We engaged in a practice assaults drill to which some zest was added by attracting some sharks."

With the temperature already ninety degrees at 8 a.m., the ocean surface was nearly glass calm as the *Pilar* headed out of Cojimar and toward the blue of the Gulf Stream. The *Pilar* plowed the only wake for miles, and soon a school of flying fish took to the air from the wave's crest. Wings beating, their slick bodies seemed to skip as easily as a flat rock across water.

"Flying fish," Gregorio called out and then added in Spanish, "Get the lines out." Paxtchi and Sinsky let out the fishing lines with baits. Don Andres, the Catholic priest, came out to the men and handed them their straw hats. Papa left the shade of the cabin and stepped out into the sun to watch the trailing lines. Fuentes had control of the helm. All hands stood watching the dark blue water behind the boat.

Bumby stood beside his father. He broached the subject of his low grades. "Look, Papa, what do grades matter—I'm going off to war soon."

"It matters if you're going to become an officer," Ernest countered.

"Fish," Paxtchi interrupted, pointing to an enormous dorsal fin slicing across a wave. The huge mako hit the far starboard line with surprising speed.

"Jesus, look at that fish go," said Bumby. He watched his father lunge to pick up the rod. The click from the right rigger indicated the small bonito bait had been savaged and, sure enough, the large shark took his meal and turned to make a run off to the port. He took an easy hundred yards of line as Bumby clicked the harness onto the reel. Papa gave two quick strikes to set the hook. It had already found its way into the shark's stomach; the big fish was gut hooked. Papa sat back in the fighting chair and watched the rod double over with the weight of the fish.

Hemingway on board the Pilar.

Hemingway's arms strained as he lifted the rod for the first pump; he reeled hard as he lowered it. Gregorio ordered Sinsky and Paxtchi to bring in the other three lines along with the two teasers.

Ernest held on to the rod and savored feeling the power of the large shark. "What a grand fish—pull, you S.O.B., show me your power." He leaned back and felt the strain vibrate the fishing rod.

"Keep on him, Ernesto," cheered Fuentes in Spanish. Bumby turned the fighting chair to a better angle, with his father facing the fish. Reeling, Papa only got in a small amount of line. Just when it looked that the line would surely break, the great shark surfaced. He was one hundred yards off port, his huge body turning slowly back toward the boat. "I've got you, you son of a bitch. He's giving up and coming toward the boat."

Everyone watched the tall gray-blue fin, a small sail moving across the ocean's calm. "No, this is a smart fish," Papa whispered as he stared in disbelief as the mako matched the *Pilar*'s speed. "You son of a whore. He's resting! Look at him," Ernest said.

Winston laughed. "What's the matter, Papa—no rest for you?"

"Never." Ernest grinned. He pumped the heavy rod and reeled in the line, trying to narrow the distance. Now the great mako began his fight in earnest. He ripped off line effortlessly and sped across the surface to the far starboard side.

"No, you don't," growled Papa, adding pressure to the drag. To everyone's surprise, the shark jumped. Full of fight, its gray-blue body twisted and flopped in and out of the water in a series of spectacular jumps and greyhounding. Fuentes kept the boat just far enough ahead, taking care that Ernest didn't lose the mako by having it snap the line.

"Should I get the Tommy gun?" asked Winston.

"Hell no. I've got him," said Ernest.

Suddenly the entire bulk of the mako's body came clear of the water and smashed down, with such force that the spray from the shark wet the transom.

Winston turned to Bumby and put an arm around him, "You know, this fish and its many brothers is why no one wants to get sunk by a sub out here."

"I agree," said Bumby.

"Note this, the mako jumps better than any tarpon or marlin," Ernest said. The naturalist in him felt tremendous love for the animal, a reaction conflicting with his primal need to exert control over the beast. After two more stunning jumps the great mako swam slow and steady as if resting. His tail swaying back and forth, he kept an easy pace with the forward motion of the boat.

"Man, think of how the Kraut bastards would love to eat this one," Ernest said.

"No, Ernesto," said Fuentes, who continued in Spanish. "These fish are demons. Free them and they turn and attack the boat. Bring them aboard and they will kill you. They are bad luck."

"Ah, Gregorio. You cannot be afraid of this fish or any fish?"

"I've seen *dentuso* dead, gaffed, brought into the boat, then alive again, snapping. My friend lost a leg to such a fish."

"We will kill the *dentuso*," Papa said, using the mako's Cuban name, given with respect to its curved-in teeth. "Wolfie, go down below and get a few grenades for the bastard to chew on. All right, men—time we practice a few things. Paxtchi, get your arm warmed up."

Assuming the stance of a major league pitcher, the tall Basque began stretching his throwing arm. Don Andres opened the egg carton Winston had brought up from below. Waving his hand in the motion of a blessing, he picked up the first fragmentation grenade for Paxtchi. The Basque made the pitch: It landed near the shark, which suddenly darted away from it.

A moment later, the water exploded. Ernest called to Paxtchi, "Going to have to do better than that!"

The big shark turned back toward the *Pilar*'s wake and moved through the churning water. Paxtchi was close enough to see the jaws open, and he threw in a second grenade. Everyone watched as the big fish swerved toward it and swallowed. The timing was perfect. A beat, and the fish suddenly exploded, white streaks of grenade dispersing into a cloud of red. A piece of the head and tail floated to the surface.

"All right, gentlemen," said Ernest reeling in the freshly broken line. "Let's see who answers our dinner bell."

It would not be hungry Germans, but many more sharks.

The crew had brought up their guns. In their Científico attire, they attacked the sharks that had come to feed on the floating remains of the dead mako. The water surface was racked by the "Rat, tat, tat, tat. Rat, tat, tat, tat" of the Thompson machine gun.

As Ernest watched the scene play out, he recalled a different time and place where he had first encountered the viciousness of sharks.

In 1935, Hemingway stood looking at the biggest marlin he had ever seen, floating just a few yards off the *Pilar*'s stern.

"He's over a thousand, isn't he, Papa?" Mike Strater asked for the second time, his voice dry and hoarse from the fight. The thought of landing such an incredible fish gave the New Englander a second wave of strength.

"He is," Ernest answered, "possibly a world record." He then glanced at his watch. "Forty minutes. You've done a hell of a great job, *el presidente*. Saca," he called to *Pilar*'s mate, "bring the gaff, we've got a world record to bring on board."

Hemingway at target practice with his submachine gun.

But as the *Pilar* closed in, the first shark appeared. He came in, striking the marlin hard in the lower flank.

"No, you BASTARDS," Ernest yelled as he fired a long burst from the Thompson submachine gun into the shark. "Rat, tat, tat, tat—Rat, tat, tat, tat, tat, tat, tat." A string of bullets splattered across the moving fin. Then the water turned red and the shark sank under the water's surface.

"Reel, goddamnit," Ernest growled. "... you don't have much time. Reel." The great marlin made a few more lunges, and it was clear he was not alone in the water. Three more shark fins surfaced and zeroed in on the wounded prize. Strater's record-size marlin met his end in a flurry of red. Ernest fired the Thompson again. Rat, tat, tat, tat— Rat, tat, tat, tat. Rat, tat, tat, tat— Rat, tat, tat, tat. The great fish lay motionless and three sharks floated beside it, their bellies raised toward the noonday sun.

"You got them, Hem," Strater cheered. "You got the sons of bitches."

"Don't be so sure, " Ernest said, squinting back at the scene. There was sudden movement by the tail of the blue marlin. "Is he still alive? My fish, is it alive? " Strater asked, reeling in the slack line.

"No," Papa answered softly.

The great fish turned over, not by its own volition but by the tugging and ripping of its flesh by two more sharks. Another shark swam between the boat and the floating fish. Strater cursed them, but there was nothing that could be done. As the *Pilar* inched closer, they could see the midsection had been chewed to the backbone, and the heavy flank meat, thoroughly apple-cored. Once again, the sharks around Bimini had won.

But in his fiction, Ernest made sure that the sharks lost:

As he shot, the clatter came again, short and tight, and the fin went under and there was a boil in the water and then the biggest hammerhead he had ever seen rose white-bellied out of the sea.

ISLANDS IN THE STREAM

Some have said that Ernest's use of the Thompson submachine gun drew more sharks to the area by releasing more blood into the water; others have argued that the Thompson's sheer shock power kept the shark attacks down. The fact is, machine gun or no machine gun, there was little chance of the sharks giving up once they had sighted the big marlin in distress. They would not relent until they had ripped all the flesh off the big fish's body. Ernest himself admitted in *Islands in the Stream* that the blood from a wounded hammerhead would call up the whole ocean. In the first few weeks of possessing the gun, Ernest had shot twenty-seven sharks, all over ten feet long. Papa felt disgust at the sight of sharks continuing to hit Strater's magnificent fish after it had been lashed alongside the *Pilar*, with Saca leaning over and clubbing at them with the gaff. It was not right for such a fish to die in this manner and while

Had it escaped the sharks, Mike Strater's marlin would have set a world record.

it had taken only forty minutes to get the fish into the boat, it would take another hour before they could hoist the remains into the cockpit.

At the dock, what was left of Strater's great blue weighed in at just over five hundred pounds. Despite being apple-cored, the fish had beaten Hemingway's own Cuban marlin record of 468 pounds for a blue. Ernest's son Patrick said that witnessing that particularly brutal shark attack was most likely the inspiration for *The Old Man and the Sea*:

"Half fish," he said. "Fish that you were. I am sorry that I went too far out. I ruined us both. But we have killed many sharks, you and I, and ruined many others. How many did you ever kill, old fish? You do not have that spear on your head for nothing." ▨

THE OLD MAN AND THE SEA

The Pilar on the hunt for German submarines.

THE REAL WAR

CHAPTER №12

When Martha returned to the Finca, she stated explicitly that the only part of the war she thought worth covering was in Europe. Refusing to take Ernest's sub patrols seriously, Martha was angered by his combat crew's dropping in at all hours of the day and night. Ernest often held practice raids: If the crew climbed through the thick undergrowth around the Finca's grounds and made it to the pool undetected, they could enjoy drinks and a swim with Ernest. But while the camaraderie was high for Ernest, Martha regarded their activities with disdain. While Ernest was occupied with his cronies, she retreated to complete her novel *Liana*.

Martha often asked Ernest to read sections of her novel, and made revisions based on his corrections. One evening, Ernest took the liberty of sharing with Winston Guest a section about a man and his wife living in a place much like the Finca. The writing described the man as always walking around barefoot, and badly in need of a bath.

"What do you think, Wolfie?" Ernest asked after finishing the chapter.

"I think she paints a rather unattractive portrait of you, Hem," Winston answered.

"Hey, Marty," Ernest called out to the bedroom, "you never said this was about me." Ernest laughed and then added, "What the hell do I care."

Martha came out of the bedroom and picked up the pages of her manuscript. "I also never said you could share it with your friends."

"Oh don't be mad," said Ernest. "I'm proud of you, daughter."

"Why didn't you mention his noble U-boat hunting?" Winston asked.

"Noble?" Martha said turning to glare at Winston. "Your sub patrols are nothing more than a fancy excuse to get gas rations for fishing. You do this while the rest of the world fights, suffers and dies. I for one am not standing for it." She shook her manuscript at both men and stormed out of the room.

Ernest and Winston turned and stared at each other. Winston began to apologize, but Ernest waved him off. "Oh forget it. Marty's..." He paused, searching for the right words to excuse her anger. "...from Saint Louis." Both men laughed, and Ernest poured another round of drinks.

Determined to report on the war in Europe, Martha could not comprehend Ernest's fixation on finding German subs.

Martha's bickering with Hemingway over his duties as a journalist continued over the next few months. He finally ended the issue, saying, "Look, Marty, go if you goddamn want to go, but there will be plenty of war left for me to get into and it will continue for a very long time." Martha finished her novel and made plans to leave for New York, and then on to London for *Collier's*.

With her bags packed, Martha came out into the Finca's living room and found Ernest and his sub-hunting crew gathered around a nautical chart on the dining table. Ernest was running his finger along Cuba's northwest coastline, the Cuban archipelagos. "Look here—the archipelagos have sixteen hundred islands and over one hundred sixty-five deep lagoons. The perfect place for a German sub to lie in wait."

Hemingway scouts the islands for German subs on the Pilar.

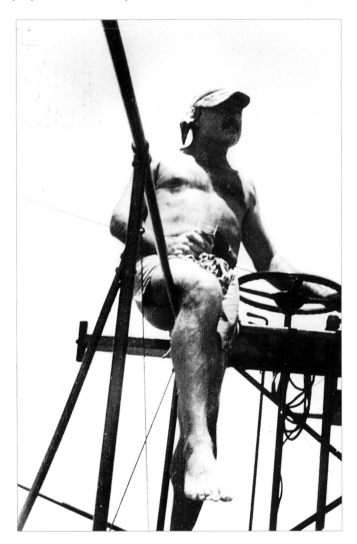

"How long will it take to get there?" asked Winston.

"Several days, but we'll stay out. We can refuel here, and here," Hemingway said, pointing to ports along the coast.

"Goodbye, Papa," Martha said from the front door. Ernest and the crew looked up from the table, and Hemingway pushed back his chair and walked over to his wife.

"Have a lovely trip, daughter," he said.

"I'll call you when I get to New York," she whispered. "And *Collier's* will get you my final address in London. "

Ernest walked Martha out to the car where his driver, a local boy named Rene, stood ready to drive her to the airport. He kissed Martha. "Be safe." She nodded and closed her door. Perhaps the anger between them had subsided, or the realization was dawning that both were now headed on very different paths, that it was time to move on with their lives.

Ernest took his sub patrol out for a three-month tour along the north coast. The seas were rough as the first northwester blew a solid white chop. Fuentes found suitable anchorage among the mangrove islands as they headed for the Romano Archipelago. Ernest spotted smoke from a fire; he took John and Paxtchi in a small skiff and went ashore and found a few turtle hunters. One confirmed that he had seen Germans approach the shoal where the fishermen cast their nets for bait. The others cited many reports of Germans going ashore looking for food and water, especially around the larger islands of Sabinal, Paredon Grande and Cayo Coco.

The next day, Ernest sent Fuentes out on the skiff to cast his net around the shoal. Fuentes returned to the *Pilar* with baitfish. Ernest pushed the *Pilar* farther along the coast, and stopped at Cayo Coco. They found a fisherman in a thatched shelter, drying his catch. There were Germans in the area, he said; just the other day he had seen six come ashore on the north face. They were in a rubber raft and left after finding water and killing two wild boars.

"We're getting closer," Ernest said when they got back to the *Pilar*. As the boat rocked in the lee of the island, he wondered if the Germans knew they were being hunted. He felt a sudden sensation of danger. Perhaps the Germans were hunting him. They could hide in any of these deep channels.

In hopes of luring the Germans to the surface, Ernest sent out Fuentes (foreground) to catch baitfish.

I know damn well this is where I would come if I were they. It is the first good place. They might have passed it and gone straight on. Or they might have turned in between Paredón and Cruz. But I don't believe they would because somebody would see them from the light and they never could get in and through there at night, guide or no guide. I think they will have gone further down. Maybe we will find them down by Coco. Maybe we'll find them right in behind here.

ISLANDS IN THE STREAM

The next morning, as the sun painted a rose hue against the clouds, the *Pilar*'s mission was again under way. They slowly passed the green and brown mangrove trees of the long key, and the islands finally opened up so they could see the ocean. The wind was still blowing and the seas were still sloppy. Another island loomed ahead and Ernest handed over the compass heading to Fuentes and went below to check the RDF. By noon, the *Pilar* had reached the island's lee and Sinsky dropped anchor. Everyone was out on deck, trying to dry out after the wet crossing.

Winston Guest saw it first. "Hem," he said pointing off to the open sea, "looks like we have a tug towing a large barge over there. It's maybe two or three miles away."

"John, get me the glasses," Ernest barked.

The marine handed up the binoculars to Hemingway. "Son of a bitch, we've got ourselves a submarine," he said looking at the water pouring from the honeycombed superstructure. He focused on the black conning tower; the hatch did not appear to be open, not yet. "Okay, let's take it nice and easy. Get your scientific hats on. Let's go see if we can make this happen, just like we practiced." He grabbed his logbook and began writing quickly all the details that he saw.

Guest took the field glasses from Ernest and looked at the craft. "Jesus, it's big."

"Okay, I want some lines in the water, so we look like we are just trolling out in the channel. Got that. Get the anchor in and Paxtchi stand by on the weapons. Okay, let's get under way."

The black hull of the *Pilar* was soon headed back out in the wet slop of the channel. The submarine was still ahead a couple of miles but progressing very slowly.

"I think we're going to catch her," Hemingway said. "Try not to look like we're doing anything but fishing."

Abruptly, one of the lines snapped off the outrigger.

"Get that, Wolfie," Ernest called down to Guest. "It's perfect. They can see we're really fishing."

Winston Guest reeled in on the line and a large barracuda shot out of the water like a missile. The fish greyhounded across the waves and kept the Englishman working to bring in line. Ernest looked out at the sub again; it was getting smaller, it was moving away from them.

"Come on, Wolfie, they're getting away. Get the fish in and let's catch up."

But even with the *Pilar*'s engines at full speed, the sub disappeared over the horizon. "Okay, take note, it was moving on a north-northwest course. Call it in."

The report was taken by the ambassador, who passed it on to the Navy. The Navy gave his report a DF rating, and Ernest was hurt that they considered his report unreliable. Two days later, when the same submarine was discovered off New Orleans trying to land four men at the mouth of the Mississippi, Ernest felt he had been proven right.

When Ernest returned to the Finca he received word of Bumby's graduation from Officer's Candidate School and his command of a platoon of MPs. He would be shipping out for Europe shortly. With his sons and wife far from the Finca, Hemingway seemed unbearably lonely. In November 1943, Ernest wrote to his first wife, Hadley Mowrer: "It is wonderful when Marty and/or the kids are here but it is lonesome as a bastard when I'm here alone. I have taught [cats] Uncle Wolfer, Dillinger and Will to walk along the railings to the top of the porch pillars and make a pyramid like lions and have taught Friendless to drink with me (Whisky and milk) but even that doesn't take the place of a wife and family."

When Martha returned to the Finca, she was finally able to convince Ernest to return with her to Europe, and Hemingway left Cuba to report on the war. ▨

The Hemingway boys visit their father in Cuba. From left to right: Patrick, Jack, Ernest, Gregory.

Mary and Ernest Hemingway at Finca Vigía.

DEAREST PICKLE
MARY WELSH HEMINGWAY

CHAPTER № 13

Ernest and Martha did not travel to London together. Both were waiting in New York to ship out when Martha was offered space on board a cargo ship scheduled to leave the morning of May 13, 1944. She would be traveling as the only passenger on the ship, which was carrying a load of dynamite. Ernest declined to join Martha on the ship, believing that its explosive cargo was an irresistible target for Nazi subs. Four days later he was offered a seat on a transatlantic Pan American flight.

Hemingway arrived in London a few weeks before Martha and found himself invited to many press parties. He complained that the thick beard he had grown during the sub patrols was now scaring off the ladies. Shortly after arrival Ernest met up with his brother Leicester and Irwin Shaw, who worked with Les in a documentary film unit. Ernest confessed to Les that though he had not initially wanted to come over to the war, he was having the time of his life. He conveyed similar sentiments in October 1944 to Max Perkins at Scribners: "I got sort of cured of Marty [by] flying. Everything sort of took on its proper proportion. Then after we were on the ground I never thought of her at all. Funny how it should take one war [Spanish Civil War] to start a woman in your damn heart and another to finish her. Bad luck. But you find good people in a war. Never fails."

True to his word, Ernest continued to meet "good people," and he lost no time finding the next keeper for his newly "cured" heart. At the White Tower, a London restaurant frequented by military and press personnel, Irwin Shaw entered with a young, petite blonde on his elbow. Her name was Mary Welsh, and she was a writer for the London Bureau of *Time-Life*.

"When will Noel be coming back?" asked Shaw.

Welsh shook her head. She had not seen her husband in months. "The *Daily Mail* has him on assignment. They think the Allied invasion of the continent is coming any day now."

"They're not the only ones," Shaw agreed.

They were ushered upstairs to a room with several tables filled with journalists. Across the room, a group of men stood talking over drinks at a bar. Shaw waved to the bearded one, and Hemingway waved back. He was dressed in his heavy wool R.A.F. uniform, having been granted permission by the Air Ministry to fly with British pilots on a bombing run.

"Oh dear," said Shaw to Welsh, "that large man with the beard is Ernest Hemingway."

"You know him?" Welsh asked. "He must be dreadfully hot in that wool uniform," she mused. "We're all bloody hot."

"Indeed," Welsh agreed, and took off her own dark wool blue jacket. Shaw's jaw dropped; Mary was wearing a very tight sweater, and very clearly without a bra. She breathed an exaggerated sigh of relief. "Ah, that's so much better."

"God bless knit sweaters," marveled Shaw.

"Oh Irwin, it's been years since I stopped being harnessed by brassieres."

"And we love you for it," Shaw said, not taking his eyes from her sweater.

"Hey, Shaw," said Hemingway, "why don't you introduce me to your friend."

Both Welsh and Shaw looked up; Hemingway stood beside the table with his very best smile.

"Oh," said Shaw, "right. Mary Welsh—Ernest Hemingway."

"Pleased to meet you," Welsh said holding out her hand.

"The pleasure is all mine," said Hemingway, and took her hand and kissed it.

In her autobiography, *How It Was*, Mary Welsh described this notable manner of meeting the man who would become her new husband. It was, for Hemingway, love at first sight; though, according to Welsh, she was put off by Ernest's sudden marriage proposal.

Shortly after Welsh returned from the restaurant to her room at the Dorchester Hotel, she answered a knock at the door to find Ernest standing expectantly. With the lights off for the mandatory blackouts, his frame appeared to fill up the entire doorway.

After a few drinks sitting on the couch together, Ernest turned to Welsh. "I know you don't know me, but I want to marry you. There is," he paused, "something about you—a vitality, an honest beauty. I am in love with you, Mary."

Welsh stared at Ernest in the darkness, trying to make out the expression on his face. Was he sincere, teasing, lonely?

Ernest took a sip of his drink. "I would marry you today, tomorrow or any day that you decide to finally fall in love with me."

Welsh still did not answer him. "You are a fine woman. Fresh, but different—like the first bite of a crisp pickle." Welsh burst out laughing. Ernest chuckled as well, pleased at the reaction. "My dearest Pickle," he said, warming up to the nickname.

"I do hope you don't think me a dill pickle," said Welsh. She smiled and then took on a more serious tone. "But you and I are married... to other people."

"I know Pickle, but things change." Ernest leaned over and gave Welsh a kiss as he stood to leave. "Sleep on it, Pickle. We'll talk again."

Welsh did not give an immediate answer to Hemingway's marriage proposal and he continued courting her with love notes. Several months later, his feelings were serious enough to issue the following request to his *Collier's* editor; Henry La Cossitt, from Hürtget Forest in Germany:

"Dear Henry: You never asked me to name a beneficiary for the insurance Colliers took out for me. I hereby name Mary Welsh of Life and Time Inc., 4 Place de la Concorde as sole beneficiary of this insurance revoking by this letter any previous beneficiaries that may have been named."

By war's end, Welsh made the decision to divorce her husband, Noel Monks, while Ernest and Martha came to the same agreement. Welsh arrived at the Finca in May and stayed for appearance's sake in a separate bedroom. They would eventually keep this sleeping arrangement, Welsh said, because of "Ernest's ungodly early morning work schedule."

Hemingway was happy to have Mary Welsh at the Finca. He showed her around and introduced her to the staff. When his cat Boise immediately took a liking to Mary, rubbing against her legs, Ernest said, "Well it's official. You can stay."

Mary decided if she was going to stay, she was going to have to learn Spanish. She had a young woman come to the Finca and tutor her in the mornings, and in the afternoons she would practice what she had learned on the Finca's staff. Slowly acclimating herself to Cuba's climate and culture, Welsh had to unlearn in some respects the fierce independence to which she had grown accustomed in London. As a Cuban Bella, she was not to have an opinion on world politics, or yearn for economic independence from her husband. It was expected that she would be taken care of by the staff of the house—much like the rest of her husband's property.

Ernest took great pride in introducing Welsh to all of his Cuban friends, especially Captain Fuentes. It seemed important to Papa to see if Mary enjoyed fishing. Reacting to the conflicts with Martha over his fishing and sub hunting, Ernest resolved on not taking a wife who did not love boating and fishing the way he did. Welsh proved herself, landing a white marlin on her first trip out. She not only knew how to fish; she demanded her own small fishing boat. "Now, here's a woman I could love forever," Ernest said to Fuentes.

On March 14, 1946, Ernest Hemingway and Mary Welsh were married in Havana, with the ceremony held at the home of Hemingway's lawyer. The drawn-out reading of the Cuban marriage contract made it apparent that the Napoleonic Code was the precursor to modern prenuptial agreements. On signing, both she and Hemingway guaranteed that should they part, everything would be returned to the original owner. Ernest's sons Gregory and Patrick signed as witnesses, along with Ernest's friend Winston Guest. Later the newlyweds enjoyed drinks at the Floridita and again at Richard and Marjorie Cooper's apartment with even

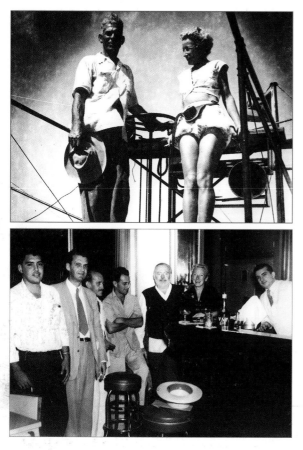

Captain Gregorio Fuentes and Mary Hemingway aboard the Pilar.

Ernest and Mary with friends at the Floridita.

more friends stopping in for toasts of champagne. When they returned to the Finca that evening, the couple began to argue, fueled by alcohol. It looked as though Mary would leave Ernest, but when they woke up the next morning Hemingway said, "Let's never get married again, Kitten."

Welsh agreed and added, "Certainly not to each other."

"Or anyone else," Ernest said and gave his bride a kiss.

Despite a rocky start, Welsh and Hemingway's union ended up lasting longer than Papa's previous marriages. Early on, Welsh's main complaint was how hard it was for her to feel that she fit into the daily life at the Finca. Nearly all of Hemingway's friends, family and staff made comparisons between her and Martha. Also, Ernest had not removed any of Martha's photographs throughout the house, claiming that he had left them up because his sons adored Martha and still missed her. Welsh finally confronted him, saying, "They adore their mothers too, but I don't see any photographs of Pauline or Hadley in here."

The point was made. Soon after, Mary and Ernest talked seriously about starting their own family. Ernest wanted more children, especially a daughter; Mary liked the idea of having a girl, and thought it would be lovely if she was named Bridget. "Short and sweet, Bridget Hemingway, or B. H. for short."

"More likely they'll call her Bridie," Ernest countered.

"Oh stop," Mary said. She went ahead with plans to turn the guesthouse into a nursery, and Ernest agreed to get a wet nurse to help her. By July, Mary was sure she was pregnant. She and Ernest left Cuba on a car ferry to Key West and planned to drive the Lincoln out west to Sun Valley, Idaho.

They never made it past Casper, Wyoming, where Mary woke up writhing and screaming in pain. Ernest took her to a nearby hospital, where they diagnosed a tubular pregnancy and discovered that the tube had ruptured. Mary's veins had collapsed from internal hemorrhaging and since she had lost so much blood, the doctors said, it was hopeless to operate.

"You had better say your good-byes," the doctor told Ernest, pulling off his rubber gloves.

"The hell I will," Ernest countered. "She's unconscious. Don't worry about anesthetic; get that damn plasma into her. Cut into the vein and hook up the IV."

"Mr. Hemingway, don't tell me how to do my job," the doctor said.

"I won't as long as you actually do it," Ernest snarled and then turned to the nurse. "Okay, you do it, or I swear I will!"

The nurse looked at the doctor, who finally gave his nod to go ahead.

"Good," Ernest said. He took his wife's hand. "Don't you give up, Pickle. You keep fighting, you hear me."

The nurse successfully placed the needle into the vein. Ernest lifted up the bag of plasma and squeezed the tubing line, running the plasma through the hose.

"What are you doing?" the nurse asked.

"Milking it," he said. "Your tubing has air bubbles in it; the vent is too tight. Got to get the bubbles out." Ernest lifted up the IV again and ran his fingers down the pinched tube to clear the line. After the first pint of plasma, the doctor reached for her hand.

He looked up, surprised, "We've got a good pulse. We've got it. Okay—prep her to operate."

The doctor and Ernest locked eyes. "Now it's your turn," Ernest said.

The doctor nodded. He was successful in removing the ruptured fallopian tube, and after four more bottles of plasma, two blood transfusions and a week under an oxygen tent, Mary was on the road to recovery.

She never forgot that Ernest had saved her life, and though at times she still missed her life in London, Mary was now happy to assume the mantle of being Mrs. Ernest Hemingway. But it took many years for her to accept her inability to produce a child. She later wrote on the subject, "At first I felt I was a slacker in the human race, being unable to contribute to it. But pining and keening couldn't rearrange my private plumbing. Later on, seeing how many of the children of my admired, intelligent friends were becoming autistic little monsters, I felt better."

Mary in a yellow convertible, one of many gifts from Ernest.

To take her mind off the matter, Ernest gave Mary more say around the Finca, especially in its decor. At first she implemented only minor changes, buying new furniture for her room, a new electric stove and refrigerator, a hot-water heater, and putting in vegetable and flower gardens around the Finca. Moving on to more ambitious projects, she went on to have the living room windows enlarged for better cross-ventilation, and helped Ernest design a lovely four-story white tower that was built between the main house and the pool. The first floor of the tower would serve as a carpentry shop; the second floor, adjacent to the patio, became the new home for the ever-increasing Hemingway cats; the third floor room, a much needed storage room; and the fourth floor, Ernest's new room for writing, with a wonderful view of San Francisco de Paula and beyond to the coastline.

Instead of a traditional sloped roof on the tower, Ernest and Mary decided on a flat roof so they could enjoy the view and Mary could sunbathe in the nude. The builders added an exterior staircase from the second floor to the third floor, and a wrought-iron spiral staircase leading up from the third floor to the walled deck. All this, Ernest thought, so the bloody gardeners wouldn't see Mary naked. Up to that point, family members and guests, including movie star Ava Gardner, had felt no qualms about swimming naked in the Finca's pool.

Ernest in his pool at Finca Vigía, a place where he felt he could relax in total privacy.

A year after they married, Hemingway began writing one of his most controversial novels. *The Garden of Eden* dealt with the moral prejudice with which society approached bisexuality. Since Ernest boasted that his characters and events were often based on real people and incidents, Hemingway readers and scholars still disagree about the origins of the bisexual character Catherine Bourne.

Hemingway began the book in 1947, but it remained unpublished until 1986, when his widow, Mary Welsh Hemingway, passed away. Much of the mystery behind Hemingway's portrayal of Catherine Bourne's bisexuality may be solved by a closer study of Welsh's autobiography, *How It Was*. Among her insights, she mentioned her desire for reversed sexual role-play in bed. She wrote that at first, Hemingway seemed to like it, but later tired of her desire to be a boy in bed.

Upon publication, several Hemingway scholars suggested that Catherine Bourne's character was based on Ernest's second wife, Pauline, and her desire to replace first wife Hadley. But aside from one obvious connection in which David Bourne and his wife, Catherine, honeymoon in the same French seaport where Ernest and Pauline honeymooned, Mary Welsh Hemingway seems to reflect more specific idiosyncrasies in Catherine's character.

In *How It Was*, Mary published a letter from Ernest saying he would agree to be her Catherine in bed, if it truly pleased her. So it may very well be that Welsh's sexual role-playing inspired this passage:

"Now can I be a boy again?"

"Why?"

"Just for a little while."

"Why?"

"I loved it and I don't miss it but I'd like to be again in bed at night if it isn't bad for you. Can I be again? If it's not bad for you?"

...“Nobody can tell which way I am but us. I'll only be a boy at night and won't embarrass you. Don't worry about it please.”

Mary loved to give small presents to Ernest and one day overheard him commenting how he loved blond hair on a woman. At the suggestion of a Cuban friend, she visited a Havana hairdresser and turned her natural honey-colored hair into a golden white. Ernest was so pleased with the transformation that Mary teased him, “Papa, you would be happiest if women everywhere had hair the color of dandelions.”

“The blonder, the lovelier, my beauty,” Ernest agreed.

To add more highlights to her blond hair, Mary began sunbathing in the afternoons on the tower's roof. Like Catherine in *Garden of Eden*, Mary became obsessed with obtaining the perfect tan.

“How dark are you going to get?”

“As dark as I can. We'll have to see. I wish I had some Indian blood. I'm going to be so dark you won't be able to stand it.”

However, Ernest showed only minor concern about Mary's sexual role-playing after she formed an unusual friendship—one that began with a car crash.

From ninety miles away in Key West, word came that Patrick and Gregory had been in a car accident. Gregory had suffered a minor knee injury, and Patrick had escaped with a scratched chin and a headache. Two days later, Patrick returned to Cuba and managed to take his College Board exams. He told his father that the headache had worsened, and Ernest correctly diagnosed a concussion. When Patrick broke out in a high fever and became delirious, Ernest called his doctor and good friend Dr. Roberto Herrera.

Ernest set up round-the-clock nursing at the Finca, giving his own bed to Patrick. He slept on a mattress just outside the door, and the Finca's staff and Dr. Herrera stayed on watch. When Pauline heard from Ernest about their son's condition she asked to come to be with Patrick.

Mary, who was out of town taking care of her father, received two letters on April 18th. One, from Ernest, explained the condition of his son. The other was from Pauline, asking her permission to stay at the Finca. “I am over here in Cuba and staying at your house,” Pauline began. “I hope you do not mind.... I was very worried about Patrick when he was in Key West.... We have a good doctor now who seems to think Patrick will get over his attack in about two weeks."

Mary reassured Pauline and urged her to use her clothes and to make herself at home. Thus began a long friendship, surprisingly unaffected by their relationships to Ernest. Perhaps it worked because Mary was not Pauline's direct successor, or simply that they shared much in common, including Papa.

As both women sat out on the Finca's porch one evening, Ernest commented, "How is it that the former Mrs. Hemingway and current Mrs. Hemingway get along so well?"

"We're alumnae of the same Alma Mater," Mary teased, Pauline laughing in agreement.

Ernest continued his work on *The Garden of Eden* and at one point even entertained himself like his character, David Bourne, by bleaching his hair. But instead of turning a lovely blond, his hair ended up the color of a new copper penny.

A few months later, Ernest sent a letter to his publisher, Charles Scribner: "Awfully sorry to have been delayed. But there has been hell's own balls up here trying to keep people from dying and all that sort of thing. But now Patrick is fine. Mary is well again and handsome and brown and happy. Pauline is staying on here with Patrick for a few weeks to finish his convalescence.... Mary will come out when finishes here. I could write probably a much better book than am writing on haveing a couple of wives around at the same time and a former and present behaveing absolutely marvellously; *really* good. But maybe will get around to that later."

But while Mary and Pauline got along splendidly, another woman would enter Hemingway's life—one that Mary couldn't ignore. ▨

Mary Hemingway and Pauline Hemingway made unlikely but good friends.

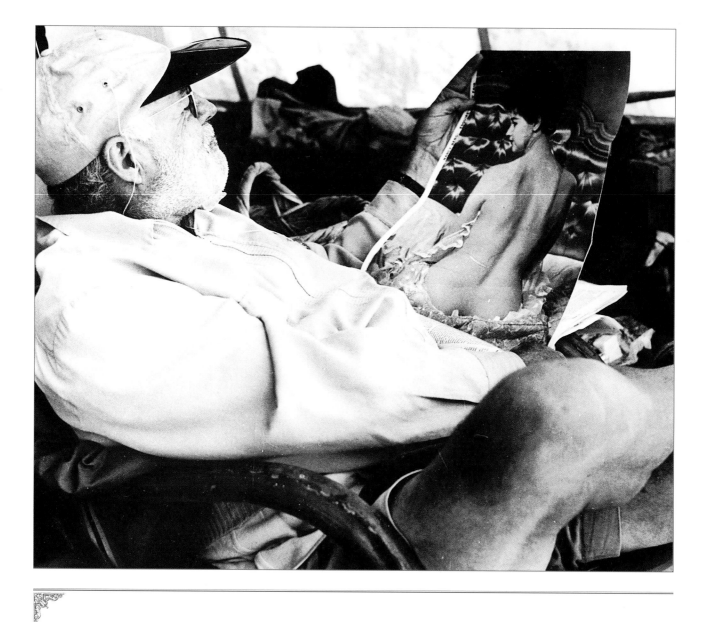

ACROSS THE RIVER AND INTO THE ARMS OF ADRIANA IVANCICH

CHAPTER №14

Shortly after Ernest celebrated his forty-ninth birthday, he decided to revisit northern Italy. Perhaps the visit was spurred by his work on *The Garden of Eden*, for which he drew upon recollections of being a young man in love. Hemingway had at that point well over nine hundred pages in longhand, and he told Mary he wanted to return to the site where he had first been wounded. Specifically, he talked about having a private ceremony in which he would defecate on the very spot where the trench mortar had exploded.

On the day Ernest drove up to the old battle site, he met a few local girls who, upon learning who he was, begged him to take them back to America. He left them at his car and walked silently over to the grass-filled depression where the trench mortar had wounded him thirty years earlier. Changing his original plan, Hemingway pulled a thousand-lire note from his wallet, bent over and stuck it into the dirt. When he got back to the car and one of the girls inquired about his curious action, he stated, "I have now given my blood and money to Italy."

After returning the young women to their homes in the nearby town of Fossalta, Hemingway returned to Venice and Mary. He wrote in the mornings, working on a story for *Holiday* magazine, entitled "The Great Blue River." He addressed a question many Italians had asked him on this trip:

People ask you why you live in Cuba and you say it is because you like it. It is too complicated to explain about the early morning in the hills above Havana where every morning is cool and fresh on the hottest day in summer.... You do not tell them about the strange and lovely birds that are on the farm the year around, nor about all the migratory birds that come through.... You do not tell them about the shooting club just down the road, where we used to shoot the big live-pigeon matches for the large money.... You could tell them that you live in Cuba because... you work as well there in those cool early mornings as you ever have worked anywhere in the world.

While Ernest seemed intent on professing his love for Cuba, it was Italy that provided Hemingway with the inspiration for his next book—and his newest love.

On a cold, wet and miserable day Ernest joined an Italian Count, Carlo Kechler, and his friends on a bird hunt. On the shoot, the group included other Italian nobility, including a young woman named Adriana Ivancich. The only woman to join the group, she had never

At the Floridita, from right to left: Gianfranco Ivancich, Adriana Ivancich, Mary Hemingway, Ernest Hemingway, unidentified friend.

Hemingway steals a glance at Adriana at the Floridita.
From right to left: Adriana Ivancich, Ernest Hemingway,
Adriana's mother Dora Ivancich, Mary Hemingway,
Adriana's brother Gianfranco Ivancich, and a friend.

ACROSS THE RIVER
AND INTO THE TREES

shot a gun prior to the trip. Adriana not only missed all of her targets; she suffered a bruise to her face by a shell casing from her own gun. That afternoon, as she sat drying out beside the great fireplace in the Kechler country estate, Ernest approached Adriana. Her face turned to him and he saw that the bruise from the casing was still red on her cheek.

"Are you all right, my daughter?" he asked in Italian.

"Not so bad—I'd be better if I had a comb," she answered, trying to smile and wincing at the pain. Her pale, narrow face seemed sad in the soft light of the fire. Ernest stared into her hazel eyes, lost for a moment. Putting down his brandy snifter, he pulled from his pocket his own comb. "Have mine, daughter," he said and gave it to her.

"Thank you, you are very kind." Her face lit up with honest joy. It seemed strange that such a simple gift as a comb would bring two such unlikely people together. Ernest was far older and wiser in the ways of the world; Adriana had been overprotected and raised as a devout Catholic. Ernest was drawn to Adriana's innocence, vulnerability, and femininity—qualities absent in Mary Welsh.

Hemingway was working on a new story that would eventually become his next novel, *Across the River and into the Trees*. What was at first a simple story about a duck hunt expanded to include his trip to the battlefield, and Ernest further reworked the story to have his hero visit the same location at two different times in his life. Without hesitation he modeled the love interest upon Adriana Ivancich and the book evolved into a love story between a nineteen-year-old woman and a fifty-year-old man. Hemingway left no question as to his subject in his description of Renata:

Then she came into the room, shining in her youth and tall striding beauty, and the carelessness the wind had made of her hair. She had pale, almost olive colored skin, a profile that could break your, or any one else's heart, and her dark hair, of an alive texture, hung down over her shoulders.

In 1950, Adriana Ivancich arrived in Cuba with her mother and her brother, Gianfranco Ivancich, and Ernest took them to dinners at the Floridita and fishing trips on the *Pilar*. Mary appeared to enjoy Gianfranco's company as much as Ernest cared for Adriana's, but she did not yet know that her husband was modeling a character after Adriana in *Across the River and into the Trees*.

Ernest took the name Renata from Renata Borgatti, whom he and his first wife, Hadley, had befriended years earlier in Cortina, Italy. The name itself meant "reborn," and Hemingway wanted his hero's love interest to represent the spirit of youth, reborn in the mind of his hero, Colonel Cantwell.

The Colonel kissed her and felt her wonderful, long, young, lithe and properly built body against his own body, which was hard and good, but beat-up, and as he kissed her he thought of nothing.

ACROSS THE RIVER
AND INTO THE TREES

Adriana claimed that she and Ernest had never consummated their affair, but at least twenty-eight of her love letters were found in the Finca's basement. When Ernest told Mary that Adriana would be coming to visit the Finca, he warned her "his heart was a target of opportunity and not subject to discipline."

Though his heart had clearly dictated the story, the reviews for *Across the River and into the Trees* were not good. Some critics charged Hemingway with losing his touch for storytelling and making the work too complicated. Ernest took the criticism as a challenge and began a new story about an old Cuban fisherman, who went out too far and caught a fish too big to bring back. 🔲

From right to left: Adriana Ivancich, Mary Hemingway, Gianfranco and Dora Ivancich.

Adriana Ivancich, Mary Hemingway and Black Dog; Hemingway and Adriana Ivancich share a private moment at the Finca.

Hemingway felt at home with the local fishermen, and lent them a hand whenever he could..

WINNING AS A CUBAN
THE NOBEL PRIZE

CHAPTER № 15

During the weeks leading up to October 28, 1954, rumors about Hemingway and the Nobel Prize ran rampant. Any talk of the Nobel put him in a foul mood and he found the new wave of speculation aggravating as ever. Ernest was still peeved at the Nobel committee, which had passed over him so many times before in favor of those he considered lesser writers. He had grumbled publicly on several occasions that the prize meant nothing, and that "no son-of-a-bitch" who won it had ever written anything worth a damn afterward. The new batch of rumors, no matter how persuasive, might be more "Bull's Milk," and Ernest worked very hard not to care about that damned "Swedish business."

To make matters worse, all the talk coming out of Stockholm speculated that the contest was boiling down to Ernest and Halldor Laxness, an obscure writer from Iceland. To compete in a field against what he thought of as no real competition was beneath him; beating out Laxness for the prize meant nothing. If he was up against Fitzgerald or Faulkner, it might have meant something. But this was a no-win situation. If he won, he would have only beaten a writer nobody had ever heard of. If he lost, again, he would lose to a complete nonentity.

Ernest and Mary often entertained friends and family in the Finca dining room.

And what if he won by a sympathy vote? Ernest was still suffering from the effects of his two African plane crashes—his back was still a constant source of pain—and the false reports of his death from the first crash had rapidly circled the globe, generating a sentiment of saccharine and even nostalgic sympathy. Winning because of that would be even worse than losing to Laxness.

The last few months had not been as productive as he would have liked. There had been too many distractions, from a visit by Ava Gardner to a report that Ernest was slated to write and star in a movie for Darryl Zanuck about hunting big game in Africa. It had taken him two days to squash that rumor, two valuable writing days, and he'd about had it with the interruptions. And Ernest knew damned well that if he actually won the prize he'd be lucky to have the time to write so much as a full sentence without a reporter trying to crawl in through the window.

With all this in mind, Ernest had done everything to build up the impression that he didn't care one way or another whether he won the prize, when in fact he had hungered for it for years. As it became apparent that he was going to win, he had forced himself to let go of all his churning resentment. He wanted to come across as gracious as he could when he accepted the prize while simultaneously downplaying its importance. But he was not in a good mood on October 28th when he emerged from his workroom. He'd been working on what he was now calling "the African Book," and the writing hadn't gone particularly well that morning. When he read the official speech awarding him the Nobel Prize for Literature, Ernest did so with very mixed feelings.

Hemingway is presented with the Nobel Prize for Literature at the Finca Vigía.

"For Christ's sake, Pickle," he grumbled to Mary as he read the presentation speech, "'pressman's catechism... use short sentences...' Ballroom bananas. Listen to this – 'instinctive predilection for grim spectacle...' they're making me a ghoul. And this – 'laconically pruned' short stories, the bastards. And I'm 'brutal callous and cynical' to boot."

"Stop it—who cares what they say? It's the Nobel Prize! You've been grumbling about it for years—and besides, I'm so proud of you." Mary chided him.

"It's going to kick off a goddamn circus and you know it," Ernest grumbled. "I won't get more than two words down on paper in the next six months."

"You'll get plenty of words down," she soothed him. "And you'll love every minute of the goddamn circus."

"The hell I will. I can't take a pee as it is without a flashbulb going off. And now this..." Mary leaned over and silenced him with a kiss. "Papa, you are the only man I know who could turn a Nobel Prize into an albatross around your neck."

"Well, hell," Ernest said. "we can sure use the money. Maybe I'll buy a goddamn airplane."

Before Mary could protest, Rene came in with drinks. Mary eased Ernest into his chair, and as he sipped, it became increasingly difficult to hold on to his bleak outlook. By the time his friends arrived to help him celebrate—well, what the hell. The Nobel Prize. Maybe it wasn't so bad, Ernest decided.

"I am very pleased and very proud to receive the Nobel Prize for Literature," he finally announced to the press laying siege at his door. And coming back inside to the jubilant party, he felt proud for his choice of words—simple and humble without being too flowery. Ernest surveyed the crowd. He had some damned good friends here in Cuba, and by God, Mary looked awfully good, moving through the packed living room of the Finca and making sure everybody got a drink and a smile. Feeling better and better, he drained his glass and pushed through the packed room to the telephone in his office. He called his pal General Buck Lanham, who was in the hospital recuperating from a hernia operation.

"Buck," he said, feeling the glow of the drinks and the enthusiasm from the party in the living room, "I just called to tell you I got that thing."

Just recently out of surgery and not yet fully recovered, Lanham at first had no idea what Hemingway was talking about. Papa finally blurted, "That Swedish thing. You know..."

"Goddamn wonderful," was Lanham's response, but when Ernest asked him to come down to Cuba and "handle me," take care of the crowds and the press and so on, Lanham declined, wishing Ernest well nonetheless.

Ernest hung up and moved back toward the party, but the phone rang. Mary pushed past him and answered. Ernest raised an eyebrow.

"Harvey Breit from New York," Mary whispered as she handed him the telephone. "He wants a quote."

Ernest gave Breit his quote, a pretty good one. "As a Nobel winner,"—by God it felt good to say that! —"I cannot but regret that it was never given to Mark Twain, nor to Henry James... Anyone receiving it must receive it in humility." Breit thanked him, congratulated him, and rang off, and Hemingway returned to the party. Several hours later, Ernest's contentment was at its peak. His Cuban friends had gathered around him, and by God they knew how to hit the right note for a celebration. In fact, everything about Cuba was great. He sure as hell would never have written *Old Man* if he'd been living anywhere else.

Ernest thought about his many friends in Cojimar, how he respected the local fishermen for their bravery, rowing and sailing their small skiffs into currents where fish of unimaginable size dwelled. He had seen everything they brought in, from huge marlin to a 7000-pound white shark, and made a point of studying their drift fishing technique, setting lines at varying depths of forty, seventy-five, one hundred fathoms deep. He had watched from the *Pilar* the way they handled their long lines, how the hooked marlin took out coils of line and pulled the small skiffs through the waves.

The ritual of admiring the catch began once the fish was hoisted from the dock to the tree beside the Terraza, where the fishermen drank together and talked about fishing. Ernest found the people of Cojimar hardworking and honest, and their lack of pretension and willingness to help each other, commendable. He thought nothing of helping the young men pull in their fishing nets or offering to tow fishing smacks back to Cojimar when seas got rough. A special relationship existed between Papa and the Cojimar fishermen and it was built on mutual admiration.

Clockwise from top left corner: Cojimar townspeople watch with anticipation as fishermen bring in their catch.

Tired Cojimar fishermen catch a ride, towed in to shore by the Pilar.

Cojimar fishermen and Captain Gregorio Fuentes (right).

Fishermen gather around the day's catch outside La Terraza, a restaurant Hemingway made famous in The Old Man and the Sea.

Filled with good cheer, he hurried outside and rounded up the staff–gardeners, chauffeur, everybody–and began plying them with drinks, drawing them fully into the party that was now spilling out onto the grounds with him. There were eleven employees at the Finca, and Hemingway had always regarded them as extended family, and as such he was determined to include them in his celebration. They were his Cuban family, and living in Cuba had finally won him his Nobel Prize. They would by God have a few drinks to celebrate with him. This turned out to be a very successful program: Not one of the staff managed to resist him and stay sober that day. Publio Enriquez, a gardener, remembered that "by the time we were done drinking I could barely find the door."

The first television interviewer arrived, a stylish young man from Cuban TV. He set up his camera in the house, and Ernest gave the interview in his careful, American-accented Spanish.

"Mr. Hemingway," the young man began, beaming at Ernest through sunglasses, "we would like to know how you feel and what you experienced upon winning the Nobel Prize for Literature."

Off-camera Ernest could see his good friends, trying to stay quiet for the interview, but nevertheless smiling and giving him the high sign. "First," Ernest answered, "I experienced a feeling of joy. And then, a little more joy–and then, a little more. I am very happy to be the first *Cubano Sato* to win this prize…"

As he stated, Hemingway considered himself a garden-variety Cuban, and his desire to give credit to the land and people of Cuba was no momentary impulse. When Ernest finally received the large gold medallion that accompanies the Prize, he presented it to the Virgen del Cobre, the national Saint of Cuba, at her shrine in Santiago de Cuba, and dedicated it to the Cuban people. 🕸

Hemingway at Finca Vigía.

ONGOING RESEARCH
AT FINCA VIGÍA

CHAPTER № 16

Finca Vigía remains the only living museum of Ernest Hemingway, meaning that the home has not changed in the arrangement of its belongings since the author was in residence. As an archaeologist regards an undisturbed tomb, Hemingway scholars feel the Finca Vigía is the final site for research, and the richest in Hemingway memorabilia.

The fact that everything inside the house remains as the owners left it, undisturbed for over forty years, makes the Finca Vigía a truly unique research facility. Of course, since everything inside the home is original and thus irreplaceable, access has been limited to a handful of dedicated Cuban scholars and invited guests. The tourists who come to the Finca are for the most part only allowed to look inside from the open windows, but this arrangement allows for scholarship and tourism to coexist.

In the past, many American scholars have bypassed the significance of Hemingway's time spent in Cuba because Cuba was not easily accessible. The Cubans have had forty years to study the contents of the Finca; ignoring their findings would be the worst kind of scholarly arrogance. Their research takes into account all of the remaining Hemingway personal papers; his letters, manuscript pages, lost years from the *Pilar*'s logbook, thousands of photographs and memorabilia. Their intimate knowledge of Afro-Cuban religion, superstitions, politics, art, music, and historical culture has revealed astounding details of Hemingway's life in Cuba.

One of the three full-time staff researchers at the Finca Vigía, Maria Caridad Valdes Fernandez, has focused her study on the connection between Hemingway's literature and the many Afro-Cubano artifacts left in the Hemingway home. Her husband, Francisco Echevarria Valdes, is the second researcher and has spent a dozen years analyzing the marginal notes that Hemingway left scribbled inside the nearly nine thousand books in his personal library. The third and final member of the team is Alberto Issac Perojo, a young man who has had the privilege of studying a four-year section of the *Pilar*'s logbook, with the boat right at hand.

With nearly forty staff members working at the Finca, the man who keeps things running smoothly is the Hemingway Museum director, Sr. Manuel

Sardinas Gonzalez. He has overseen the daily operations of the Museo Hemingway for the last few years, and kept the house open for both serious scholarly study and the thousands of Hemingway tourists who make their way daily to the San Francisco de Paula home.

Maria C. Valdes Fernandez is an expert on the Afro-Cuban religion of Santería; her official title is Head of the Cultural Extension Department on Hemingway Research. Maria's work is twofold; first, to make Ernest Hemingway's life and work accessible to everyone from schoolchildren to adults. This work often involves helping many of the local schools organize theater skits and art projects that feature Hemingway themes. She also promotes the students' performances of the skits at the Finca Vigía during the year. The museum displays the children's artwork in the second-floor room of the white tower.

The second part of Maria's work is her ongoing research on Hemingway's interest in African and Afro-Cuban religions and culture. It is well known that Hemingway had converted to Catholicism, but most Americans are unaware that Hemingway had an understanding of Santería, and may have practiced it. Catholicism and Santería are two of the unofficial religions of Cuba. The latest studies suggest that many Cubans practice some form of the Santería rituals. Santería has grown in popularity by successfully merging Catholic tradition with African/Yoruba folklore.

Hemingway always made a point of taking careful observations of the cultures he depicted in his writing. When he worked on the manuscript that later became *True at First Light*, he did everything he could to accurately portray the life of a Masai warrior, learning to hunt with spears, the rituals for taking a wife, and gaining an understanding of Masai language and culture. According to one story told by the staff of the Finca, his treatment of the Santería practices was no less methodical.

Hemingway had given orders that no one was ever to prune or disturb in any way the ceiba tree in front of the house. The giant tree was believed to be at least one hundred years old, and measured over eight feet in diameter. A few years after the war, when Mary moved into the Finca, she noticed a new bump on an old straw rug that Martha had bought. Lifting the rug, she discovered that a root from the old ceiba tree had crossed under the house and pushed itself through the tiles in search of water.

"Don't you dare touch that root," Ernest told Mary, walking up behind her.

"You can't be serious?" Mary said picking up the broken pieces of tile. "If it were cut even with the floor, we could reset it with new tile."

"The hell you will," Ernest said. "Nobody will cut this bloody root."

"But people will trip over it," Mary protested.

"Then let them fall."

"You're being unreasonable, Papa."

"Look," Hemingway said pointing out the window. "All this is, is that the lovely old ceiba is thirsty. When it finds no water—the root will recede. Got it?"

Mary shook her head and stood up. "You're incorrigible."

A few days passed, and Ernest left the house to go into Havana. Mary watched as the car drove down the driveway and out the gate. Then she sent a message to a young man who lived outside of San Francisco de Paula. She specifically wanted someone who was not close to Ernest and who would have no problem removing the root.

The Finca Vigía staff was surprised when they overheard Mary instructing the man in Spanish, "My husband is an irritable tyrant. You had better work fast." The young man did as he was told and after a couple of swift whacks of a machete, the root was free in his hands.

"I said," Ernest growled, appearing suddenly at the front door, "I did *not* want you messing with my goddamn tree root!"

Mary froze; the young man dropped the root to the floor and ran out the back door of the guest room. Ernest gave chase and managed to get off a shot from his 12-gauge shotgun. Luckily, it was intended more to scare and he clearly aimed at the sky.

In the religion of Santería, the ceiba tree is the home for the Orishas, or gods. It is said that the city of Havana was built around one of these trees. The roots of the ceiba resemble fingers on a hand reaching out. Offerings are made to appease the Orishas, and are placed on the roots of the tree. When worshippers leave prayers to be answered, they are folded and placed in the crooks and cracks between the dirt and roots, in the manner of prayers inserted in the cracks of Jerusalem's Wailing Wall.

Today, this severed piece of ceiba root is one of many religious relics that sit on shelves in the library next to two lion skulls. Ernest reportedly made Mary serve a penance for her misdeed; kneeling in front of the ceiba, she was to ask its forgiveness over the course of a week.

The root is one of almost two dozen religious relics from Africa and the Afro-Cuban religion of Santería left in the house. As we entered the library to examine the others, I noticed yet another root hanging down like mistletoe from the arched entry, and asked Maria about it.

Hemingway considered sacred the ceiba tree outside his bedroom window.

"That is a mangrove root, placed there to prevent the demons from the sea from going into the air and entering. Understandably, the most important thing for Hemingway as a writer was to keep his books safe. As you can see, there are books all over the house, but most are concentrated here. So the root is for protection of his library."

Leaving the library we moved on to the guest room where Maria showed us more religious relics from Africa. On the top of one of the bookcases sits a Wakamba tribe death mask, a tusk from a wild boar, a beaded bracelet, a Masai tribe ceremonial headdress and a Masai bowl made to carry fire in the rainy season and water in the dry season. But perhaps most telling is a Kenyan voodoo doll, supposedly presented to Ernest by an old witch doctor.

A tribal mask and one of Hemingway's many cats.

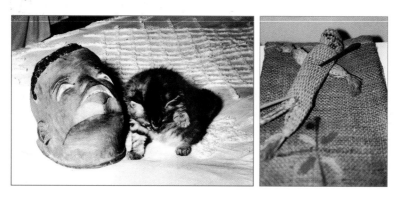

Ernest placed this voodoo doll near his books.

"It is not placed here merely for decoration," Maria said, pointing to the woven cloth doll on the shelf. "The doll is made of fibers and within the weave are two laces, one of red and one of yellow. The way it works is that for every person who might want to hurt Hemingway, these laces were to reject and protect him from injury. I think also he chose to keep it on this bookshelf because he wanted his guests to use the library without stealing any of his books. As you know, Hemingway made many notes in the margins indicating his own criteria on the writer and book, and this notation was known only to him, and not to any other person. This doll is here to protect him and his library."

On closer examination, I had to agree that no guest would steal a book from a library guarded by a voodoo doll with needles impaled in the groin and heart.

The last place we looked for African artifacts was Ernest's bedroom. A small Kudu skin lies on the floor, on the spot where Ernest would stand for hours at a time, early in the morning, typing. Toward the bathroom and placed above a matador's red cap are thirteen knives. Maria indicated the war trophies and gifts, and those for ceremonial purposes, ornately decorated with cowrie shells. Next to the knives, Maria pointed out the canes. "These canes," began Maria, "came from the African tribal chiefs of the Wacamba and Masai tribes. They are made of the regla tree, a mystical tree in the African religion Babalu-Aye, and the sticks are also associated with the Santería god, Chango. Of course, you can find walking sticks in the Catholic religion with Saint Lazarus, the saint who walks with a cane surrounded by ducks. He has had great influence on the Cuban culture and we have a day to celebrate this saint's life, on December 17th."

As we leave Ernest's bedroom, I asked Maria if she thought Hemingway was a superstitious man.

"Absolutely," Maria answered, and then pointed to a bowl of good luck trinkets just below the head of an African buffalo mount. I saw more shells, an old rabbit's foot and a lucky stone.

My father, Leicester, had explained, "All writers, fishermen and sailors are superstitious. They know inspiration and luck is like faith—God given, but without it you're screwed."

Hemingway once explained that he had been very religious when he was a young man in the First World War, and had converted to Catholicism after his second marriage. But he lost some of his faith during the Spanish Civil War when he found that the church had sided with the enemy, and by the end of that war, he said he had stopped praying altogether. "It seemed somehow crooked to have anything to do with a religious institution so closely allied to Fascism."

By World War II, Ernest had grown so cynical about God, particularly during war, that when a division chaplain came over to him, Ernest asked him, "Chaplin, do you still believe there's no atheists in foxholes?" And the chaplain answered, "No, sir, not since I met you and Colonel Lanham."

But two years before the end of his life, Hemingway told his friend Gary Cooper, "I still believe in belief." Perhaps Hemingway found other avenues and religions in order to exercise that belief.

Francisco Echevarria Valdes, head of the Finca's Library Research, contributed to the debate.

"I've been working with the library of the house, which is the most important collection of all. The value of the books is great, because they are very old editions, rare editions, and because they have all these notes that Hemingway wrote inside the margins. Some do not necessarily relate to the text of the book, even though others do. Mainly they're notes, where he used the blank space of the book to write about the activities he did. Hemingway was always reading. If he went fishing, he had a book with him. If he went hunting, he had a book with him. If he was drinking, he had a book with him. And he would write about the things he was thinking he wanted to do—or had just done. A note about the fish he just caught, or the weather situation, even his health. There's a lot of information in these books, which can be a primary source for all the people who are interested in studying Hemingway."

As I looked over the floor-to-ceiling bookcases, I asked Frank to name the most insightful piece of margin writing that he had found thus far in his research.

"That's very difficult, for me to pick just one. In my work I'm trying to group all the notes according to their content. And for instance, the ones that give you more information about Hemingway are those where he writes about the things he was going to do. Even projects, or the contents of letters he wanted to write, or telegrams he was to send to family or friends. And also you can see at times he was trying to control his expenses. He would make notes to himself on what he spent money on."

Frank thumbed through a book from the shelf. "Here, this was interesting. It seems that this day he decided he would not drink any alcohol. So he began by writing down everything he drank that day and at what time. In the morning, a cup of water, coconut water, afternoon citrus juice and at the end of the day—whiskey," Frank said and laughed.

"It is like a revelation. To be able to see the real story, right here." Frank thumbed through the pages so I could see the marginalia throughout the book.

One of the most sought-out books of Hemingway yet to be published is the complete log book of Hemingway's fishing boat the *Pilar*. I spoke with Alberto Issac Perojo in his office by the Finca pool.

Inside the office are dozens of biographies, and filing cabinets filled with research. Besides working on the *Pilar*'s ships logs, Issac, as he calls himself, is the Head of Research of Incoming Letters to Hemingway. He has held this position since 1988, organizing several thousand letters left behind in the basement of the Finca Vigía. Most of these letters were sent by everyday people asking Hemingway for his autograph, a photograph, or permission to use excerpts from one of his novels, but there are also letters from close friends like Adriana Ivancich and the movie star Ingrid Bergman.

But Issac's time in the past few years has been largely occupied by his research on the *Pilar*'s ships logs. These log books cover the years 1941, 1942 and 1943, the time during which Hemingway focused his energy on his Crook Factory submarine patrol. I asked him if he had seen any documentation of the German U-boat sighting. When he replied no, I told Issac that in the other logbooks kept at the John F. Kennedy Library in Boston, Carlene and I had seen an entry in which Hemingway and Winston Guest had spied a surfacing Nazi submarine.

As we walked past the pool toward the wooden decking that now surrounds the *Pilar*, I asked Issac why he thought Hemingway's work is so important to the Cuban people. He flashed a smile and answered carefully.

"They say Hemingway lived here in Cuba because this is the place where he won the Pulitzer Prize and Nobel Prize for Literature, but Hemingway himself said he lived in Cuba because it was the closest place to the ocean he wrote about. I think it was also because he got along so well with the Cuban people. He had many friends here in San Francisco de Paula, and also in Cojimar and here he was treated like he was another Cuban. People used to call him Papa, or El Gringo, with love. If someone in town was sick, and they were from a poor family, Hemingway would offer money for a doctor. He helped build the school in this town. He cared about the people and they cared about him."

Hemingway shows a guest a mistaken report of his death in an airplane crash.

THE HEMINGWAY PROJECT
RESTORATION OF THE FINCA VIGÍA PAPERS AND MUSEO HEMINGWAY

CHAPTER № 17

Remember to get the weather in your god damned book—weather is very important.
- Hemingway to John Dos Passos

The dark gray clouds moved in fast over the hills and the rain came down in hard sheets. An average midafternoon thunderstorm, but the potential for damage at the Finca sent the staff hurrying for buckets and plastic tarps. They spread the tarps over the bookcases and the beds, and placed buckets where the plaster in the ceiling had given way to a steady stream of water. Finca Vigía, like so many other buildings in Havana, needed a new roof, new plumbing and a new coat of paint. But the repairs were postponed indefinitely after Hurricane Michelle, a category 5 storm, came roaring across the breadbasket of central Cuba in November 2001, leaving the country in a state of emergency. Money set aside for restoration projects such as the Finca was reallocated to buy food for the Cuban people.

Several months later, in January 2002, Jenny and Frank Phillips visited Finca Vigía for the first time. The granddaughter of Max Perkins, Hemingway's longtime editor at Scribners, Jenny hoped that she would find part of her grandfather's legacy within the Finca. "I didn't know if they would have heard of Maxwell Perkins," said Jenny. "But their immediate reaction was, Yes, that's an important link, why don't you come back tomorrow for a special tour."

The Phillips did return, and they spent hours wandering through the house, looking at Hemingway's clothing, listening to his music, and thumbing through the books of his library. "It really was quite wonderful," Jenny said. "There's nothing sanitized about it. I think that's the benefit of it, as well as the problem. Because the windows are open all day long, the tropical air, the humidity and sun causes things to break down."

"Of course, we really wanted to find anything that was left by Max Perkins—any letters, or books," added her husband, Frank Phillips, the State House bureau chief for the *Boston Globe*. "Perkins sent Hemingway tons of books and you can still find them in the library. They also had letters from Perkins. We asked if we could see them or get descriptions of the contents; and we ran into an impasse."

The curators were hesitant, explaining that permission from the Cuban Minister of Culture, Abel Prieto, was required in order to obtain access to the letters. The Phillips returned to Boston and met with Megan Desnoyers and Deborah Leff of the John F. Kennedy Library, trying to find the right approach to the situation. "It became very clear to us," Frank said, "that this really was a political issue. I've covered Massachusetts politics for thirty years and I thought we could solve it through political routes. To make a long story short, we hooked up with Congressman Jim McGovern from Massachusetts, one of the leading advocates for normalizing relations between the United States and Cuba. He immediately grabbed hold of this; he was very excited about this project."

A month later the Phillips returned to Cuba to meet with members of the Ministry of Culture, Abel Prieto and the director of the Cuban National Heritage Council, Marta Arjona. They reached an agreement, and with the guidance of Gladys Rodriguez Ferrero, former director of the Hemingway Finca Vigía Museum and current director of Hemingway Studies at Havana's Institute of Journalism, their plan became a reality. As the sole curator of the papers for over twenty years, Gladys was the first to catalog and organize the material. She had understood the value of the material early on and had requested to restrict access to prevent further damage to the papers.

The agreement allows American conservators to work with their Cuban counterparts to repair and preserve all of the Finca papers; additionally, it permits scanning and microfilming of the collection into an electronic copy for the John F. Kennedy Library, while the originals remain in Cuba.

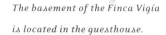

The basement of the Finca Vigía is located in the guesthouse.

"We all love Ernest Hemingway," Gladys said, "his passion for life, and the beauty of his writing—that is what this agreement is about."

Since the Hemingway Society has yet to review the contents of the Finca collection, the following are only general descriptions of what we saw in the Finca's basement, which was clean and dehumidified, with a tiled floor and freshly painted walls. In total it holds some two thousand letters and more than three thousand photographs, all of tremendous interest to Hemingway scholars, along with the marginalia in the nine thousand books of Hemingway's personal library. His comments range from opinions on the text at hand to thoughts for use on his future work. About 20 percent of his books have underlining, comments or margin writings.

Among the two thousand letters, two stand out as particularly surprising in their revelations.

In one, Hemingway writes to his younger sister, Carol Gardner, after he returns from World War II. Much has been written about the relationship between Ernest and Carol Hemingway. After she married John Gardner, Ernest had cut off all communication and emotional attachment to her. Despite his disapproval, Carol remained happily married to Gardner for the duration of their lives. In the letter, which he never mailed, Hemingway points out that the only course of action he felt he could take was to shoot Gardner, but expresses regret for his actions and says that he missed her. The letter details the impact of the war on Ernest, his son Bumby, and their brother Les, and how Les had proved himself in Ernest's eyes. Finally, Hemingway goes on to reveal that he had finally "cured" himself of Martha, realizing he needed someone more invested in being his wife than in being a writer.

In the second letter, Ernest tells Martha how the war affected Bumby, who lost fifty pounds in the POW camp, and assures her that Bumby was slowly gaining back the weight in Cuba. He reveals how they both talk about her with affection, that he suspects that all his sons would always love her. Ernest remarks that their split has been mutually respectful, and received very respectfully by shared friends in literary circles. Filling her in about the news in his life, he gives details of his car accident and the injuries he and Mary sustained, and reassures Martha that they are both fine. After discussing some divorce matters, Ernest ends on a supportive note, wishing her well in her writing. He wrote the letter in response to a letter from Martha in the same file folder, but it is believed that Hemingway never sent the letter.

Many scholars have wondered why Hemingway never mailed these letters; some speculate that his new wife prevented him from mailing them out of a deep-seated insecurity that would affect their relationship to the end. Scott Donaldson, Hemingway scholar, biographer and president of the Hemingway Society, said regarding Mary Welsh Hemingway's tendency toward jealousy, "Their marriage I think was difficult, troubled and got very difficult toward the end. I know there are things in Sun Valley they haven't gone into yet and other women were involved and I think more and more is going to be coming out, people are working on books on that relationship.

Many other treasures await assessment in the Finca's basement: an early draft of *For Whom the Bell Tolls*, galleys of *Across the River and into the Trees*, Hemingway's war medals, two rifles and, most intriguing, twenty-six letters written in Italian from Adriana Ivancich, who served as the model for the heroine in *Across the River and into the Trees*.

The basement contains Hemingway's papers, photographs and other personal items.

Dr. Gerald Kennedy, Hemingway scholar and vice president of the Hemingway Society, stated of Ernest's relationship to Adriana, "What we can infer from Mary's diary is that there was a very close, probably intimate relationship between [Hemingway and Ivancich], although Hemingway was suffering from so many physical problems at that point in his life, including occasional impotence; it's hard to speculate…. There is a famous pattern of one wife for each major novel with each wife being identified and courted before the previous marriage broke up. I think it's fair to say Adriana was an important influence in the same way. Providing a certain amount of sensual excitement in his life, an attraction that provided inspiration to write. I think he really fed off that, whether or not there was anything going on with them in the bedroom."

In the center of the basement, a long wooden table houses Hemingway items neatly filed in folders: photographs, some taken by Robert Capa during the Spanish Civil War; a poetry anthology in which Hemingway circled "No man is an island," a line from John Donne's poetry that would serve as the epigraph to *For Whom the Bell Tolls*; a page with a one-line epilogue to *For Whom the Bell Tolls*, which Ernest later rejected; Hemingway's personal copy of the screenplay for the motion picture *The Old Man and the Sea*, marked with his notations. The papers range from complete manuscripts to scraps of paper, including one where Ernest penned a profanity-laced dialogue between soldiers during World War II. He eventually dropped it, writing at the top of the page, "too frank."

Another file holds a series of love letters between Mary and Ernest, and subsequent missives indicating that the relationship was struggling. In one note, Ernest details the events that transpired during a weeklong argument: a misunderstanding over negotiations with *Look* magazine, Mary waking him in the middle of the night with a scolding, her public displays of anger, fits of jealousy over other women. Ernest debates whether he should give up his hopes for an idyllic marriage, whether he needs to learn not to care.

A copy of *Wuthering Heights* reveals records Ernest kept of his daily weight and blood pressure, which seems to correspond to the three-year record of his weight on his bathroom wall. One notation reads, "215 lbs. Oct 7, 1957 (After NY, 17 days off diet—5 drinking.)"

Letters from Mary to the Finca's staff give specific directions for preparing and presenting food, and warn them not to disturb Ernest while he is writing.

In another folder, Hemingway carefully saved the international newspaper articles about his presumed death in two different plane crashes in Africa in 1954. Hemingway also kept Michelin maps of Spain, scribbled with names of people he met and restaurants and hotels he visited, details he wished to remember for his writing.

Sean Hemingway, the official spokesperson for the Hemingway family, attests, "The Finca papers represent a chance for scholars to gain a better understanding of my grandfather and his work; we won't know the extent of its significance until this material has been studied."

Thanks to the hard work of many people on both sides of the Gulf Stream, the Phillips returned to Cuba with a delegation of Hemingway scholars, curators and members of the Hemingway family on November 11, 2002, for a formal ceremony. Congressman Jim McGovern gave the opening remarks.

"This is an extraordinary moment for all of us. We are gathered to announce and to celebrate a historical collaboration agreement between the people of Cuba and the people of the United States.

"We're honored to have a part of that legacy here with us this morning. Members of the Hemingway family join us: Sean Hemingway, the grandson of Ernest Hemingway; and his wife Colette; Ernest's daughter-in-law Angela Hemingway and his niece, Hilary Hemingway. I'd also like to take a moment to recognize and to thank all the people of the U.S. delegation who have worked so hard to make this day a reality. Jenny and Frank Phillips, Dr. Sandy Spanier from Penn State University, Deborah Leff from the John F. Kennedy Library in Massachusetts, Ann Russell from the Northeast Conservation Center and Eric Hershberg from the Social Science Research Council.

"I mentioned that we all share a love for Ernest Hemingway. But I also have another passion. I believe that the Cuban and the American people have been kept apart for far too long by politics, rhetoric and mistrust. I have a passion for tearing down those unnecessary walls and for building a new relationship based on communication, exchange, trust and mutual respect.

"And even today, forty years after his death, Ernest Hemingway can help us achieve that goal. He was an American through and through, but he also loved this country and its people and the Cuban people loved him back. That includes all of the people here in Cuba whose mission it has been to care for this amazing collection of documents, books, photographs and other materials."

The ceremony was held beside the Finca swimming pool.

From left to right: Congressman Jim McGovern, President Fidel Castro, Jenny Phillips, Gladys Rodriguez Ferrero, Director of Hemingway Studies at Havana's Institute of Journalism, Director of the Cuban National Heritage Council Marta Arjona, Frank Phillips.

The congressman then introduced Sean Hemingway, who spoke on behalf of the Hemingway family.

"In 1961, my grandmother Mary Hemingway gave to the Cuban government the Finca Vigía and its contents in an arrangement with President Castro. We thank the Cuban government and the many individuals who have honored that gift by maintaining this historical and literary landmark where we are today. As a museum curator myself, I am very aware of the constant care and diligence that such a job entails. The historic project that is inaugurated today is an important step toward ensuring the preservation of this extraordinary collection for future generations. I'm sure that my grandfather, who loved this country where he lived and wrote for so many years, would be so very pleased to see this important collaboration between the United States of America and Cuba. Thank you."

Sean Hemingway, speaking on behalf of the Hemingway family.
Background from left to right:
Eric Hershberg of the Social Science Research Council,
Minister of Culture Abel Prieto, President Fidel Castro.

Finally, Jenny Phillips stood before the audience.

"For me this is a personal event because in some ways it is helping me connect with my grandfather, Max Perkins, Hemingway's close friend and editor. Max Perkins loved Ernest Hemingway very much. He loved the man and he loved the writer. He was dedicated to the protection and carrying on of Hemingway's writings. So I'm here as a representative of my grandfather.

"When I walked in that house I was aware that the Cuban people had protected the legacy of Ernest Hemingway. His spirit still resides in this house. You feel as if he just stepped out to go down the driveway to go pick up the mail. And at a meeting in the Ministry of Culture two days ago in translating into English someone used the verb *treasuring*. They said we've been treasuring this heritage. It doesn't quite translate into English and that's the point because treasuring is a Cuban spirit and that's exactly what the Cuban people have done. So I very much look forward to working with all of you in any way that I can. Thank you."

The agreement signed by Marta Arjona, director of the Cuban National Heritage Council, and Eric Hershberg, program director of the Social Science Research Council, a New York–based nonprofit organization, laid out an arrangement under which the documents will be preserved and copied by digitalization and microfilm. Additional funds are being raised to repair the Finca Vigía buildings and restore the *Pilar* from termite damage. The Phillips hope to raise $500,000 through donations to fund the project; with the help of Megan Desnoyers of the John F. Kennedy Library, an initial grant of $75,000 was secured from the Rockefeller Foundation to begin the restoration project.

A surprise guest waited his turn to speak at this historic agreement, his presence marked by the arrival of guards at the Finca Vigía grounds armed with submachine guns. I had dozens of questions I wanted to ask him, and he answered one. Why, through the Cold War and the embargo, had Fidel Castro kept alive the memory of my uncle, an American writer? 🔲

President Fidel Castro, Gladys Rodriguez Ferrero, Marta Arjona.

Jenny Phillips, granddaughter of Max Perkins, Hemingway's longtime editor.

Background from left: Eric Hershberg, Abel Prieto, President Fidel Castro.

Ernest Hemingway and Fidel Castro met for the first and only time at Hemingway's fishing tournament.

CASTRO & HEMINGWAY

CHAPTER № 18

There has always been speculation about Hemingway's leftist leanings, even allegations of Communist sympathies, stemming from Ernest's support of the Loyalists during the Spanish Civil War. Between the Communist-supported Loyalists, and the Fascists, who were backed by the Nazis, he believed he had chosen the lesser of two evils. Ernest Hemingway hated the Nazis, and he was not a Communist. In a letter to Max Perkins in April 1931, he wrote, "Let business be a little bad and <u>everyone</u> is spooked about communism. Personally I dont like it as a regime to live under."

Toward the end of his life, Hemingway drank heavily, suffering from clinical depression and, some believed, paranoia. He told his wife Mary and his friend A. E. Hotchner that he believed the FBI had him under surveillance, and as it turned out, Papa was correct. The Federal Bureau of Investigation did keep a file on Ernest Hemingway, and its 127 pages reveal intense scrutiny of Ernest's activities, with many pages of blacked-out lines. The remaining text shows that the FBI's interest in Hemingway started after he raised support for the Loyalists during the Spanish Civil War. For the next twenty years, J. Edgar Hoover attempted to vilify Hemingway as a Communist. Ernest was in good company; the FBI was investigating many well-known American writers of his time. When Ernest formed the Crook Factory in 1942, Hoover tried repeatedly to shut it down, to no success, and increased surveillance on Hemingway.

Castro did not announce the communist nature of his revolution until well after it had succeeded, and everything known about the bearded revolutionary at the time seemed positive: He was considered honest, well educated with a respectable family; many of Ernest's Cuban friends knew him and thought well of him. Outspoken in his opposition to corruption, Castro stood in stark contrast to Batista, whose astonishing corruption and brutality compelled Hemingway to view any change in the government as a positive step. Batista's troops had tortured and murdered several young men Hemingway had known from the Finca's neighborhood, leaving their bodies in nearby ditches. In an infamous incident, a Batista soldier had also killed Ernest's beloved pet Black Dog. When Castro succeeded in forcing Batista into exile, Ernest remarked to his friend A. E. Hotchner, "I just hope to Christ the United States doesn't cut the sugar quota. That would really tear it. It will make Cuba a gift to the Russians. You'd be amazed at the changes. Good and bad. A hell of a lot of good.

After Batista any change would almost *have* to be an improvement."

Evidently, Hemingway supported Castro, but the other side of the coin was more ambiguous. Why did Castro seem to care so much about Ernest Hemingway? Why did he choose to keep the memory of this American author alive? Castro had only once previously spoken in public about Hemingway. Footage of that event exists, in the care of the University of the Arts in Havana, but the audio track to the 16-mm film was lost.

Above: President Fidel Castro and Minister of Culture Abel Prieto. Below: President Fidel Castro addresses the assembly.

On the day of the ceremony, no one knew that Fidel Castro was coming to the signing. His presence upon arrival was overwhelming to the point that everything else seemed to recede into the background. When invited to speak, he answered many questions that lingered about his relationship to Hemingway. His speech, brief by his standards, lasted half an hour— an off-the-cuff remark for Castro, who has been known to give long spontaneous speeches. He began by praising Hemingway's legacy.

"I must express my gratitude to Hemingway for many things. First, because a great author bestowed on us the honor of choosing to live in our country and writing some of his major works here. I am also grateful to him for the great pleasure that I experience reading his books. He is one of the greatest authors that ever lived.

"I have never read anything like *The Old Man and the Sea*. One of Hemingway's greatest qualities as an intellectual—as an author—was the way he presented his monologues. If asked what I liked best about his writing, I would say his monologues, found practically in all of his work. But the best of them all is that small narrative, *The Old Man and the Sea*, about a man alone in the sea, talking to himself, meditating, reflecting on life, dreaming and struggling—to reach the end of his endeavor with only the remains of the big fish he caught.

"We cannot really call his work novels or fiction.... I learned history reading Hemingway," Castro said. "*A Farewell to Arms* is history. *For Whom the Bell Tolls* is history. I learned from Hemingway many things." He shared his thoughts on Hemingway's submarine hunts during World War II, referencing parts of *Islands in the Stream*.

"You should not believe that the attempt to catch the submarine was fiction," Castro said. "Anyone who is familiar with the psychology of this writer, his history and his life knows that it is not fiction that he writes.

"I have something else for which I am grateful to Hemingway. His work *For Whom the Bell Tolls* had a significant influence on my life personally. I had to put into practice an idea in order to face a very complex political situation in our country. We started from scratch, basically; we had no weapons, no guns. We had to solve the situation of how to defeat a regime that had seventy to eighty thousand well-armed and well-equipped men, and a government that had international support and seemed invincible. How could we face that situation when all other legal and constitutional avenues had been closed to this country and its citizens?

"I remembered from [*For Whom the Bell Tolls*] the point where the entire plot developed. A small patrol of cavalry behind the front line draws near to an area where combat is taking place; a man with a machine gun watches that patrol unit from a distance. In our history there is the story about a feud between the farmers and the landowners who had evicted them from their land. A journalist explained that in such places one man, well placed, could stop an army. I have always kept in my memory Hemingway's descriptions of what happens behind enemy lines. It was an awakening.... I have never forgotten that book."

President Castro moved his hands along the microphone and cable. He paused before continuing, gathering his thoughts.

"What is a man without history?" Castro continued. "Without history we would not even have an idea of how limited the work of the human species is. The human species continues to make mistakes all the time. Just a few days ago, we had a visit here from a very well known American filmmaker, Mr. Steven Spielberg. He showed his films in a small festival, one of them the very impressive *Schindler's List*, which is a

From left: Minister of Culture Abel Prieto, President Fidel Castro, Dr. Sandy Spanier, Jenny Phillips.

very well known film in our country. Seeing how great historical monuments are destroyed— the big statues, the Buddhas that were destroyed in Afghanistan—I wonder whether mankind has really reached any degree of civilization. On the other hand, when reading data about the tremendous destruction of nature taking place every day, you see that man is destroying his own habitat, in addition to all the beauty of nature and all the fishes which are already in danger of extinction.... You wonder, are we really civilized? I wonder, too, whether man has the necessary capacity to survive his own actions.

"When you meditate and reflect on that, you feel more admiration for a man like Hemingway. It is true that he liked big game hunting. His grandson [Sean Hemingway] presented me with a book about his grandfather and big game hunting in Africa. I asked him, how do the environmentalists feel about this? He said, Well, these are new times, we cannot redesign

Hemingway to fit into these times because in his day he criticized the hunting of men and the massacres of the war. At that time there was no awareness about the need to protect nature, so many men were killing animals; there were no environmentalists."

Fidel reminded the crowd that, although he had always thought very highly of Hemingway, they had not known each other very well on a personal level.

"I had very few chances to meet Hemingway," the president explained. "But in 1959 I was invited to take part in Hemingway's marlin fishing tournament, and he was there. It happened by chance that after three days, I caught a huge marlin, which gave me first place. One might suspect that somebody put the fish on the hook for me, but that was not the case... and it was Hemingway who presented me with the Cup."

One of the most famous series of photographs in Cuba captures the moment when these two men met. Prints of Hemingway and President Castro are everywhere in Cuba—hanging

above the bar, on walls in hotel lobbies, proudly displayed in private homes, the two most famous beards of their time, chin to chin, grinning at each other.

"I would have liked so much to have had the time to talk with him," continued Castro. "But this has happened more than once in the course of the last forty years. You feel that you have all the time in the world, that people will be there forever for you to talk to them. Many times I have received the news of a death of a person I meant to talk to... and that happened to me with Hemingway. In my office I have a picture of Hemingway with an enormous marlin, what must be the marlin of *The Old Man and the Sea*.

"I have told you about my personal relationship with Hemingway, my affection, my admiration for him. Of course his words will live much longer than any of us. The work of art lasts for thousands of years."

Fidel gestured toward the agreement.

"The contents of the document which has been signed move me very deeply. We do not deserve all the recognition expressed in the words of the speakers here today, but we have made the effort to preserve Hemingway's documents and the house which today is a museum."

Castro pointed back toward the Finca. "I think we would be savages if we did not recognize the importance of preserving this place. We do not deserve the recognition; we simply behaved in a civilized fashion."

A sea of faces gathered around Hemingway's empty pool, all listening intently to Fidel Castro. It was a group Ernest would have approved of—a diverse collection of humanity represented by Hemingway scholars, businessmen, Finca Vigía staff personnel, politicians, Hemingway family members, and the granddaughter of his editor.

Fidel wondered out loud how Hemingway might feel if he were present. "I think," Castro concluded, "he would have fun watching this ceremony, perhaps even writing something about what has happened today. I hope all of us can write the story together as he might have written it himself."

Castro leaned over the table and signed the historic document. A few moments later, I found myself signing just above his signature. ▨

President Castro signs the agreement.

from left: Dr. Sandy Spanier, Frank Phillips, Hilary Hemingway, Gladys Rodriguez Ferrero.

HEMINGWAY'S CUBA TODAY

CHAPTER № 19

San Francisco Wharf

There will be a day when American cruise ships will join the fleet of European ships already making port along the two-story terminal at the San Francisco Wharf. Today, as it was during the time when Ernest lived in Cuba, a large cobblestone plaza stands directly across from the wharf. But it no longer is filled with sailors and fishermen; now an upscale destination, it caters to the ever-increasing number of tourists. A uniformed officer trains his eyes on the tourists entering the square. Ubiquitous in Havana, uniformed police officers seem to be on every corner, which is no doubt one reason Havana boasts the lowest reported crime rate in all of the Caribbean.

An opening riff on conga and bongos signals the start of lunchtime music. A five-piece salsa band starts up for the gathering crowd at a large outdoor café at the north end of the square. The far side of the square is lined with elegant and newly restored three- and four-story buildings. *La Perla,* or the Pearl Café, where Ernest set the opening shootout scene in *To Have and Have Not,* once stood among these buildings, but was torn down in the 1950s.

Most of the buildings that remain in the square now keep businesses on the first floors, including restaurants, cigar stores and art galleries; the upper floors are residential. Due to a serious housing shortage, many Cuban residences may have several generations of the family living under the same roof, often sleeping two or three to a room.

Hotel Ambos Mundos

Less than a mile from the San Francisco Wharf, the Hotel Ambos Mundos is the first place Hemingway stayed in Cuba. A five-story building built in 1920, the Ambos Mundos was one of the first buildings to be restored with the UNESCO funds. It now sports a fresh coat of paint the vibrant pinkish-orange color of a conch shell's underbelly, and sits on the cross corners of Calles Obispo and Mercaderes in the heart of old Havana. The hotel has retained its open-air lobby, with floor-to-ceiling doors so that cool sea breezes flow through year-round. Guests awake to the sound of horse-drawn carriages on the cobblestone streets, the smell of fresh

brewed coffee and the aroma of an occasional Cuban cigar.

In the lobby during most hours of the day, a woman plays on the baby grand piano, accompanied by a violinist. Opposite a café with chairs and tables on the far side of the bar, clerks wait eagerly at an oak desk to greet guests. Across from the desk, local artists place block prints and watercolors of Havana scenes and prints of Hemingway on a large coffee table. A locked glass case features trinkets, including porcelain table dinner bells with Papa's portrait and locally printed T-shirts.

Ambos Mundos literally means "of two worlds," and the phrase describes old Havana perfectly. Almost 150 buildings in the old city date back to the sixteenth and seventeenth centuries. But the Hotel Ambos Mundos seems to best define its own name, with its turn-of-the-century antique elevator and air-conditioning units in each of the rooms. Cubans are surprisingly sharp on marketing and commercializing Hemingway. Fortunately, they devote an equal amount of enthusiasm to honoring the man and his work, almost to the point of reverence.

Hemingway wrote descriptions of the hotel in letters to friends: "At this Hotel Ambos Mundos you can get a good clean room with bath right overlooking the harbor and the cathedral—see all the neck of the harbor and the sea for $2.00." Today the tour price of Hemingway's room 511 remains $2 dollars. It can be viewed most hours of the day by making an appointment in the lobby. The hotel also offers a guided tour by a Cuban expert on Hemingway, Ms. Esperanza Garcia Fernandez.

Esperanza gives tourists a quick summary of Papa's life and work while walking through the small room containing a roped-off bed, an antique dresser, photographs and a few of Hemingway's books, locked in a china hutch. A chair and desk with an old typewriter sit in the center of the room. Esperanza swings open the window's shutters, showing the view Papa enjoyed and allowing a cool sea breeze to fill the room. Even after Hemingway bought his home Finca Vigía, he continued to keep his room at the Hotel Ambos Mundos for visiting friends.

The view from his window remains much as Papa described it for *Esquire*: "The rooms on the northeast corner of the Ambos Mundos Hotel in Havana look out, to the north, over the old cathedral, the entrance to the harbor, and the sea, and to the east to Casablanca peninsula, the roofs of all houses in between and the width of the harbor. If you sleep with your feet toward the east, this may be against the tenets of certain religions, the sun, coming up over the Casablanca side and into your open window, will shine on your face and wake you no matter where you were the night before."

Many have wondered why Ernest Hemingway preferred to stay at the Hotel Ambos Mundos over Cuba's more famous establishments, such as Hotel Nacional, once known for its world-class casino as well as its rich and famous clientele. But Hemingway enjoyed his privacy and liked being in the heart of old Havana. He found the Ambos Mundos pleasant not only because it was close to the wharf, where he kept his fishing boat, but also for the spectacular view, which still includes the red tiled roofs of the city, the dome of the old cathedral built by the Jesuits, and the mouth of Havana Harbor, with its lighthouse and the El Morro fortress.

The only place with a view better than Hemingway's room is the roof just above it, where the Hotel Ambos Mundos offers a rooftop bar. The bar did not exist during the time Ernest rented his room; had it, he might never have left to explore the rest of Havana. The view at night is truly spectacular and the drinks are always strong.

One of Cuba's most famous drinks is the mojito, a rum beverage with a punch like a first-round heavyweight knockout. Though Hemingway enjoyed mojitos, he preferred another Cuban drink at a watering hole just up the street.

The Floridita

The Floridita Bar & Restaurant sits on a corner of Calle Obispo, with a red, white and blue neon sign hanging above the front door. Ernest immortalized the Floridita in his novel *Islands in the Stream* as a setting for his character Thomas Hudson to soak his sorrows after the loss of his sons in a tragic car accident. Ernest himself did a good amount of soaking at this nightspot, often meeting friends and fellow writers for drinks. In 1953, the Floridita ranked in *Esquire's* top bars of the world, a list which included the 21 Club of New York, the Ritz in Paris and Raffles in Singapore.

Today, the Floridita has a roped-off section at the end of the bar, marking a small shrine for Saint Ernesto featuring—what else?—his bar stool. On the wall above the chrome throne hangs a bronze bust and several large photographs of Papa with various celebrities.

The Floridita remains one of Havana's top tourist draws. Tour buses drop off groups just outside the door. Everyone enters intent on one thing—drinking a *Papa Doble*. While sitting on Papa's throne is not permitted, ordering his famous double daiquiri is almost mandatory. The bar has changed significantly from the open *bodega* Ernest fell in love with in the 1930s. Even by the late '50s, Papa commented that the place had "gone too upscale," with "too many of those damn tourist types." It remains one of the most popular places to eat and drink in Havana.

Old Havana

About noon a parade makes its way through Old Havana, intended to catch the attention of the tourists. It begins at the Plaza de Armas and continues along Calle Obispo, men and women walking on tall stilts and dressed in colorful costumes, playing drums. Like giant

living puppets they dance down the street, stopping traffic and spreading smiles to young and old alike. The streets of Havana have a wonderful mix of colorful characters, from made-up clowns to men and women dressed in traditional Spanish garb posing with cigars, dancing with tourists. Like the characters in American theme parks, they are there for the visitors' benefit, but it is not a realistic image of the working people of Havana—the fishermen, truck drivers, students, garbage collectors, bartenders, doctors, maids, taxi drivers, cooks—the people who keep the city going.

The back streets of old Havana have been described as a time capsule. What we see at the start of this new millennium is not very different from what Ernest saw when he wrote about this Caribbean city. Past the old buildings, a chorus of *Guantanamera* rises from a café. Brightly dressed musicians play on a mixture of bongos, maracas, guitars and a six-string instrument called a Trey.

Most of the streets, too narrow for cars, have been blocked by heavy cast-iron balls the size of huge cannon balls. At midday the streets are packed with a stream of humanity. Most are men and woman in their twenties and thirties fighting to make a buck at various jobs. Some are considered black market enterprises by the Castro government. The hustlers or, as they are called by fellow Cubans, *jineteros*, try to sell the tourists bogus cigars, cheap rum and young women. But with the typical government job paying an average of seven to ten dollars a month, Cubans have learned to supplement their income either through the black market, or from family living in the states.

Since the Soviet Union stopped its financial support of Cuba, the island's economy has foundered. One of the ways the Castro government employed to pay bills was cashing in on the tourism trade. Today, tourism surpasses the island's sugar crop as one of Cuba's main industries. But with tourists come everything that the communist leader claimed were the evils of his predecessor, Batista. There is now a rise of haves and have-nots. Those individuals in the tourist industry earn significantly more money. It is no wonder that many people, even doctors, work at least part-time in the expanding tourism trade. Many make more money as part-time artists or musicians than they could ever make in their government jobs. A typical musician might pull in twenty-five dollars a night while a doctor working for the government will make twenty-five dollars a month. The result: music spills out of every small café, bar, restaurant and hotel lobby in Havana. And while I was attracted to the sounds of Havana, Ernest made a point to describe the smells. In *Islands in the Stream*, he wrote of the smell of newly opened flour sacks, roasting coffee and fragrant cigars.

Havana Harbor

At the time Ernest fished in Havana harbor, many more billfish swam close to shore than do today, though young Cuban fishermen still arrive in the early mornings to fish off the Malecón, Havana harbor's famous promenade. They come equipped with rods and reels, and Cuban yo-yos—handheld spools of line. They float out on makeshift rafts, some that are just blocks of Styrofoam, or more commonly, a truck tire inner tube.

The best way to enjoy the view of Havana harbor by land is to walk along the Malecón. Young couples and families meet on the extra wide sidewalk and seawall for lunch breaks, and in the evenings, lovers of all ages go to enjoy the sunset and mingle. The Malecón marks a stretch of colonial buildings painted in fading pastel colors of pink, green, orange and blue. The buildings are still handsome from a distance, but up close cry out for repair.

The harbor's water quality is being restored, enough so that many Cubans fish the waters for dinner. I passed a young family sitting along the dock's seawall. The father held his young son while keeping an eye on the fishing line leading from the water to a Coke can, a poor man's version of a Cuban yo-yo. The mother cut up a fresh mango and offered a bite to her husband. Daily life for many Cubans is much like fishing. You don't know what you'll have for dinner, but casting the line brings hope. The Cubans I met remain hopeful. Most of the population of Havana lives in extended family homes; in order to survive, families must pool their money to buy life's staples—black beans and rice. For many families living in the cities, meat, usually pork or chicken, is eaten only once or twice a month, since it is expensive.

Travel for tourists remains relatively easy and inexpensive compared to other metropolitan cities. For less than five dollars, you can take a taxicab across town. Taxis range from brand-new Mercedes to vintage '50s American autos to small Russian makes, and bright yellow Coconuts—colorful vehicles that run like golf carts. For visitors swept by the romance of the city, there is also the horse and buggy. The genuine antique carriages

re-create the experience of traveling in the 1700s, from the clip-clop of the hooves to feeling the bumps and bruises of real cobblestone roads, without shock absorbers.

A ride along the harbor's entrance turns toward the large twin towers of Hotel Nacional, passing faded pastel art-deco apartments, some with old men sitting in doorways with cigars. Across the street, bobbing in the water just beyond the famous Malecón promenade, men drift in large black inner tubes. Using Cuban yo-yos, they drift-fish for mutton snapper. Out beyond the fishermen lies a small fleet of fishing smacks. The men here are long lining; this is a lucky fishing area and they are fortunate to have fish in close to shore.

Finca Vigía

The high point of the Hemingway trail is visiting Ernest Hemingway's Cuban home, the Finca Vigía, literally "lookout farm." The lovely Moorish-style home is located at the top of a hill in the town of San Francisco de Paula. Though modern tour buses slowly wind up the narrow streets of the town to drop off tourists, the public is not allowed inside the house,

which contains the original belongings of Hemingway. Ernest's personal library of nine thousand books, his furniture, the animal heads, even the artwork– including a Picasso plate of a bull–still hangs on the walls. Ernest's slippers lie beside his bed, his reading glasses rest on the night table. His small portable typewriter stands ever ready for the next day of hard prose. Every item in the home is accounted for and in every room a security guard keeps watch. Most tourists are not allowed to enter the house, and are led in groups around the perimeter of the house to peer in from the windows. There are occasional private tours of small groups that are permitted to step within the house. Our group had the pleasure of hearing a reading by Gertrude Stein on one of Ernest's old phonograph records. It reconfirmed that Ernest did in fact keep his interest in the expatriates of his Paris years. Perhaps listening to Gertrude inspired him for his work on the book *A Movable Feast*.

We moved freely through the house, stopping to listen to one of the curators speak about some of Ernest's favorite singers and how many of the books in the library are copies autographed by the authors. Ernest kept copious notes in the margins of these books, some brief—"This is great," "Oh balls;" other notations are longer and are being compiled by the Cuban researchers for publication. Among the personal papers the Cuban scholars are working to preserve are letters and manuscript pages left behind by Mary Welsh Hemingway, four more years of the *Pilar*'s log book and a never-before-published afterword to the novel *A Farewell to Arms*.

The main house looks almost exactly as it did when Martha Gellhorn found it in 1939. Today the roof leaks, evidenced by the water-stained plaster on the ceiling. The building, like most in Havana, needs plaster work and paint, but with the new agreement to restore the Hemingway papers, there are plans to repair the house and Hemingway's beloved boat.

Just outside the house stands the four-story white tower, which Ernest designed to have a spectacular view and privacy for writing. Curiously, Papa rarely wrote in the tower, saying it was too quiet; he missed the sounds of the house. The tower did become the main residence for Papa's beloved cats. Today, the second floor displays schoolchildren's art featuring various scenes from *The Old Man and the Sea*; the third floor exhibits the remaining fishing artifacts—among them a broken deep-sea rod, heavy marlin lures, and many photos of Papa fishing. Inside his writing room on the fourth floor is a writing table, chair, and lion skin rug.

Coming down from the main house, a shaded sidewalk leads to the large pool. Since the museum cannot afford chemicals at this time for the pool, Papa's favorite swimming hole remains empty. Beside the pool are the graves of Ernest's dogs, complete with headstones. There are no markers for his many cats; some say Ernest was superstitious and did not want the cats' graves marked. It is believed that his cats, including his beloved Boise, are buried in the garden under a tree outside the dining room door.

Past the pool lies sadly one of the hardest hit Hemingway artifacts, the *Pilar*. For years it has rested in the permanent dry dock on the Finca's old tennis court. Surrounded by tall green bamboo trees, the boat has become home to a huge colony of termites, which have eaten their way through the old oak-planked hull for over a decade. But since termites eat from the inside out, the exterior of the boat still looks wonderful. The hull still gleams with her high-gloss black paint, and inside the cockpit the mahogany deck has been restored to the original dark wood color, from the lime green Ernest had painted her in the 1940s. Restoration work is finally under way and Carlene and I were allowed on board for a tour, brief but thrilling especially for Carlene, an avid big game angler.

The interior cabin, painted bright yellow, revealed two bunks in the bow, and a small galley with icebox and sink. A dinette folded into another set

of bunks. The head, too small to sit and close the door, obviously was not intended for women. The cushions looked new, and apart from piles of termite dust, the boat seems in fine condition. The *Pilar* sits on cement blocks, like Noah's ark waiting for the flood.

Cojimar

The fishing village of Cojimar lies nine miles from the Finca. A small Spanish fort guards the mouth of the harbor, now home to the Cuban military. Down from the fort are the remains of an old pier where Ernest kept the *Pilar*. Today the pier sits broken from the mainland. Teenage boys from Cojimar swim out to the slab jutting out from the water, climb up, and take running dives off the end. The very first monument dedicated to Ernest's memory stands across from the pier. The fishermen of Cojimar each contributed a small bronze cleat or old propeller to be used when the artist cast the bust, in memory of their friend.

A few hundred feet from the monument is La Terraza Restaurant, where the character Santiago brings in the remains of his epic fish in *The Old Man and the Sea*. I looked out the window just as the American tourist had in the novel, and saw below the weathered pilings of the old dock mentioned in the book. I could almost picture the skeleton of the great fish in the shallow water. Dining at La Terraza is truly a wonderful experience.

Cojimar was also the hometown of Ernest's mate, Captain Gregorio Fuentes. Carlene and I had the pleasure of meeting with him before he died at age 103. Fuentes became the incarnation of Santiago as he aged. In November 2001, I presented Fuentes with the IGFA Captains Hall of Fame Award. As I gave him a kiss on the cheek, he looked just as Ernest described Santiago:

"The old man was thin and gaunt with deep wrinkles in the back of his neck. The brown blotches of the benevolent skin cancer the sun brings from its reflection on the tropic sea were on his cheeks...

Everything about him was old except his eyes and they were the same color as the sea and were cheerful and undefeated."

THE OLD MAN AND THE SEA

Sadly, Fuentes died in January of 2002 from cancer, but like Santiago, he lived his life on his own terms—honest and true. ▨

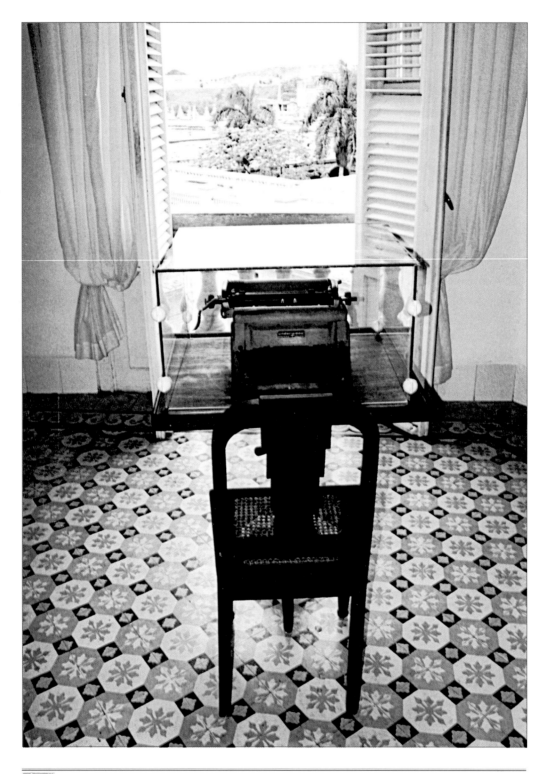

YOU COULD TELL THEM THAT YOU LIVE IN CUBA BECAUSE...
YOU WORK AS WELL THERE IN THOSE COOL EARLY MORNINGS
AS YOU EVER HAVE WORKED ANYWHERE IN THE WORLD.

"THE GREAT BLUE RIVER"

ACKNOWLEDGMENTS

Scholars of Hemingway are known for assisting each other with research and we owe a great debt to many scholars in Hemingway studies who have contributed to our work over the past several years. We are especially thankful for those who helped us with interviews, photographic research, specific studies in the Cuban Hemingway collection of archives and memorabilia, access to the historical locations in Cuba that Hemingway frequented, and the ongoing research being conducted at the Finca Vigía, Museo Ernest Hemingway in San Francisco de Paula.

In Cuba these individuals are: Abel Prieto, Cuban Minister of Culture; Marta Arjona, director of the Cuban National Heritage Council; Gladys Rodriguez Ferrero, the director of Hemingway Studies at the Institute of Journalism; Manuel Sardinas Gonzalez, the director of Museo Ernest Hemingway; the Research Staff at Finca Vigía: Francisco Echevarria Valdes, Maria Caridad Valdes Fernandez, Alberto Issac Perojo. Also, Danilo M. Arrate Hernandez; Guiomar Venegad Delgado, professor of drama at the University of the Arts in Havana; Esperanza Garcia Fernandez, historian at Hotel Ambos Mundos; Denise Jacques, wife of the Canadian ambassador to Cuba, who graciously opened to us her home, the former estate of Jane and Grant Mason. Thanks to Ernest's good friend Captain Gregorio Fuentes, and to Majel Reyes Iuesada, who has become like a daughter to us.

In the United States, we are grateful for the support and interviews granted by members of the Hemingway family, in particular to Patrick and Dr. Carol Hemingway, Dr. Sean and Dr. Colette Hemingway, Mina Hemingway, Angela Hemingway, Rosalie Hemingway, John Hemingway, John E. Sanford and Dr. Gregory Hemingway. Additionally, we wish to thank Megan Desnoyers, Deborah Leff and Stephen Plotkin of the Hemingway Collection at the John F. Kennedy Library in Boston; Allan Goodrich and James Hill of the audiovisual archive at the John F. Kennedy Library; Lydia Zelaya at Simon & Schuster; Michael Katakis for his advice regarding Hemingway foreign and film rights. Appreciation also for the generous assistance of Scott Schwar, executive director of the Ernest Hemingway Foundation of Oak Park, and of Dr. Luis Vasquez of MILA Tours, who first showed us the beauty of Cuba.

We would like to acknowledge and thank the individuals who made the historic Hemingway papers collaboration agreement a reality: Jenny Phillips, Max Perkins's granddaughter; her husband, Frank Phillips; Congressman Jim McGovern from Massachusetts; Ann Russell from the Northeast Conservation Center; and Eric Hershberg from the Social Science Research Council.

For insight and interviews, we thank the following Hemingway scholars: Dr. Sandy Spanier,

Penn State University; Scott Donaldson, biographer and immediate past president of the Hemingway Society; Dr. Gerald Kennedy, vice president of the Hemingway Society; Dr. James Nagel, the University of Georgia; Dr. Linda Wagner-Martin, the University of North Carolina and president of the Hemingway Society; Dr. Jack Crocker, Florida Gulf Coast University.

For generously granting us use of transcriptions of interviews with Hemingway scholars and President Fidel Castro, we acknowledge WGCU-TV, and especially the support of Dr. Kathleen Davey, Tim Kenney, Sheri Coleman and Lori Jennings. Thanks to Gail Morchower, librarian of the International Game Fish Association's Fishing Hall of Fame Museum in Dania Beach, Florida.

We would also like to recognize Kathy Beekman, owner of Sanibel Island's Moto Photo, her staff Jerry Sherman and Tommy Holt for their expertise, and Hollie Smith, proprietor of Sanibel Island Book Shop, who kept the research books coming – our very own Sylvia Beach.

We thank our husbands, Terry Brennen and Jeffry P. Lindsay, and others who have given invaluable assistance on this book: Dr. August and Tommie Freundlich, Shamie Kelly, Captain Trey and Jana Barclay, Bill and Shirley Semmer, the Semmer Electric staff, Ayita Rainey, John Richard, Joanne Semmer, Lorraine Baldwin, Betty Hill, Annie Brennen, Scotty Brennen, Beryl Gray, Tommie Hemingway Mulder, and Dr. Leroy and Maxine Henderson.

Special thanks to Randy Wayne White, whose friendship brought us together; to our literary agent, Peter Rubie, whose valuable assistance and advice made this book possible; to our publisher, Shawn Coyne, who believed in our book; to our publicist, Tammy Blake, for her guidance; and to our editor, Lady Chris Min, who was our Max Perkins, traveling with us to Cuba and Boston and giving us advisory and supportive editorial expertise. 🕮

PHOTO CREDITS

THE ERNEST HEMINGWAY PHOTOGRAPH COLLECTION
JOHN FITZGERALD KENNEDY LIBRARY, BOSTON

1, 2, 4, 8, 10, 11, 12, 13, 14, 16, 17, 18 *bottom*, 22, 25, 26, 27, 32, 33, 34
37, 40, 41, 42 *top*, 44, 49, 51, 52 (© Coral Gables News Bureau), 53, 55, 56
58 *bottom left*, 59, 61, 62, 63, 64, 65 (Fla. State News Bureau), 66, 67 *bottom*
68, 69 (Fla. State News Bureau), 71, 72, 74, 76, 77, 78, 79, 80, 82, 83
86, 87, 88, 89, 90 91, 93, 95, 96, 97, 98, 99, 101, 102, 103, 106, 107 *left*,
108 (Hans Malmberg, Stockholm), 111, 128, 133.

CARLENE F. BRENNEN

3, 5, 7, 9, 15, 18 top, 19, 23, 43 *right*, 58, 67 *top*, 107 *right*
113, 114, 116 *bottom*, 117, 118, 121 *bottom*, 122, 123, 124, 125, 126, 127, 128
129, 130, 131, 132, 134, 135, 136, 137.

INTERNATIONAL GAME FISH ASSOCIATION
DANIA BEACH, FLORIDA

42 *bottom*, 43 *left*, 45.

THE ESTATE OF LEICESTER HEMINGWAY

16, 104, 105, 109, 110, 115, 119

PERMISSIONS

Reprinted with permission of Scribner,
an imprint of Simon & Schuster Adult Publishing Group, from
ERNEST HEMINGWAY: SELECTED LETTERS, 1917-1961,
edited by Carlos Baker. Copyright © 1981
The Ernest Hemingway Foundation, Inc.

Reprinted with permission of Scribner,
an imprint of Simon & Schuster Adult Publishing Group, from
ERNEST HEMINGWAY: SELECTED LETTERS, 1917-1961,
edited by Carlos Baker. Copyright outside the United States:
© Hemingway Foreign Rights Trust.

From ACROSS THE RIVER AND INTO THE TREES
by Ernest Hemingway. Copyright © 1950
by Ernest Hemingway. Copyright renewed © 1978
by Mary Hemingway. Reprinted by permission of Scribner, an
imprint of Simon & Schuster Adult Publishing Group.

From FOR WHOM THE BELL TOLLS
by Ernest Hemingway. Copyright 1940
by Ernest Hemingway.Copyright renewed © 1968
by Mary Hemingway.

From THE GARDEN OF EDEN
by Ernest Hemingway. Copyright © 1986
by Mary Hemingway, John Hemingway,
Patrick Hemingway, and Gregory Hemingway.

Reprinted with permission of Scribner,
an imprint of Simon & Schuster Adult Publishing Group
from ISLANDS IN THE STREAM
by Ernest Hemingway. Copyright © 1970
by Mary Hemingway. Copyright renewed © 1998
by John Hemingway, Patrick Hemingway,
and Gregory Hemingway.

Reprinted with permission of Scribner,
an imprint of Simon & Schuster Adult Publishing Group from
THE OLD MAN AND THE SEA by Ernest Hemingway.
Copyright 1952 by Ernest Hemingway.
Copyright renewed © 1980 by Mary Hemingway.

From "The Short Happy Life of Francis Macomber,"
in THE SHORT STORIES OF ERNEST HEMINGWAY.
Copyright 1936 by Ernest Hemingway.
Copyright renewed © 1964 by Mary Hemingway.

Reprinted with permission of Scribner,
an imprint of Simon & Schuster Adult Publishing Group
from TO HAVE AND HAVE NOT by Ernest Hemingway.
Copyright 1934, 1937 by Ernest Hemingway.
Copyright renewed © 1962, 1965 by Mary Hemingway.

Reprinted with permission of Scribner,
an imprint of Simon & Schuster Adult Publishing Group
from BY-LINE: ERNEST HEMINGWAY,
edited by William White. Copyright 1933, 1936, 1949
by Ernest Hemingway. Copyright renewed © 1961, 1964
by Mary Hemingway and By-Line Ernest Hemingway, Inc.

Reprinted with permission of Scribner,
an imprint of Simon & Schuster Adult Publishing Group
from THE ONLY THING THAT COUNTS:
The Ernest Hemingway-Maxwell Perkins Correspondence,
edited by Matthew J. Bruccoli with the Assistance of Robert W.
Trogdon. Copyright outside the United States: © Hemingway
Foreign Rights Trust. Quote printed with the permission of The
Ernest Hemingway Foundation.

BIBLIOGRAPHY

Arnold, Tillie. *The Idaho Hemingway*. Buhl, Idaho: Beacon Books, 1999.

Baker, Carlos. *Ernest Hemingway: A Life Story*. New York: Charles Scribner's Sons, 1969.

Baker, Carlos. *Hemingway: The Writer as Artist*. Princeton, N.J.: Princeton University Press, 1952.

Bell, Brian, ed. *Cuba*. Boston: Houghton Mifflin Company/ Insight Guides, 1995.

Berg, A. Scott. *Max Perkins: Editor of Genius*. New York: E. P. Dutton, 1978.

Brian, Denis. *The True Gen*. New York: Grove Press, 1988.

Bruccoli, Matthew J., ed. *Conversations with Ernest Hemingway*. Jackson, Miss.: University Press of Mississippi, 1986.

Burgess, Anthony. *Ernest Hemingway*. New York: Thames and Hudson, 1978.

Cagner, E., and Tre Tryckare. *The Lore of Sportfishing*. New York: Crown Publishers, Inc. 1976.

Calder, Nigel. *Cuba: A Cruising Guide*. St. Ives, Cambridgeshire, England: Imray Laure Norie and Wilson, Ltd., 1997.

Carr, Virginia Spencer. *Dos Passos: A Life*. Garden City, N.J: Doubleday and Company, Inc., 1984.

Donaldson, Scott ed. *The Cambridge Companion to Ernest Hemingway*. New York: Cambridge University Press, 1996.

Donnelly, Honoria Murphy with Richard N. Billings, *Sara and Gerald*. New York: Holt, Rinehart and Winston, 1982.

Dos Passos, John. *The Best Times*. New York: The New American Library Inc., 1966.

Farrington, S. Kip, Jr. *Fishing with Hemingway and Glassell*. New York: David Mckay Company, Inc., 1971.

Field and Stream, eds. *The Sportsman's World*. New York: Henry Holt and Company, 1959.

Funcia, Claudio Isquierdo. *Hemingway: Poor Old Papa*. Habana, Cuba: Ediciones Mec-Graphic, Ltd. 1995.

Finney, Ben. *Feet First*. New York: Croven Publishers, Inc., 1971.

Foss, Cline. *Fidel Castro*. Phoenix Mill, Great Britain: Sutton Publishing, 2000.

Franklin, Jane. *Cuba and the United States: A Chronological History*. New York: Ocean Press, 1991.

Fuentes, Norberto. *Ernest Hemingway Rediscovered*. New York: Charles Scribner's Sons, 1988.

Fuentes, Norberto. *Hemingway in Cuba*. Secaucus, N.J.: Lyle Stuart, Inc. 1984.

Gellhorn, Martha. *The Face of War*. New York: Simon & Schuster, 1959; New York, Atlantic Monthly Press, 1988.

Gellhorn, Martha. *Travels With Myself and Another*. New York: Eland, 1978; New York: Penguin Putnam, 2001.

Gentry, Curt. *J. Edgar Hoover: The Man and the Secrets*. New York: W. W. Norton, 1991.

Gingrich, Arnold. *The Well-Tempered Angler*. New York: Alfred A. Knopf, 1973.

Goadby, Peter. *Saltwater Gamefishing Offshore and Onshore*. New York: TAB Book/McGraw-Hill, 1991.

Grey, Zane. *Tales of Swordfish and Tuna*. New York: Harper & Brothers, 1927; Lanham, Md.: Derrydale Press, 1991.

Hemingway, Gregory H. *Papa: A Personal Memoir*. Boston: Houghton Mifflin, 1976.

Hemingway, Jack. *A Life Worth Living*. Guilford, Conn.: The Lyons Press, 2001.

Hemingway, Jack. *Misadventures of a Fly Fisherman: My Life With and Without Papa*. Dallas, Texas: Taylor Publishing, 1986.

Hemingway, Leicester. *My Brother, Ernest Hemingway*. New York: World Publishing, 1961; Sarasota, Fla.: Pineapple Press, 1996.

Hemingway, Mary. "Hemingway." *Look*, September 12, 1961.

Hemingway, Mary Welsh. *How It Was*. New York: Alfred Knopf, 1976.

Hemingway, Valerie. "The Garden of Eden Revisited: With Hemingway in Provence in the Summer of '59." The Hemingway Review, 18, no. 2, Spring 1999; Moscow, Idaho: University of Idaho Press, 1999.

Hotchner, A. E. "Papa Hemingway." *The Saturday Evening Post*, March 12 1966.

Hotchner, A. E. *Papa Hemingway: A Personal Memoir*. New York: Random House, 1966; New York: Carroll & Graf, 1999.

Kert, Bernice. *The Hemingway Women*. New York: W. W. Norton and Company, 1983.

Kiley, Jed. *Hemingway: An Old Friend Remembers*. New York: Hawthorn Books, 1965.

Lawrence, H. Lea. *Prowling Papa's Waters*. Marietta, Ga.: Longstreet Press, 1992.

Leff, Leonard J. *Hemingway and His Conspirators*. London Rowman & Littlefield Publishers, Inc., 1997.

Ludington, Townsend. *John Dos Passos: A Twentieth Century Odyssey*. New york: Dutton, 1980; New York: Carroll & Graf Publishers, Inc., 1998.

Lynn, Kenneth S. *Hemingway*. Cambridge, Mass.: Harvard University Press, 1987.

Martin, Linda Wagner ed. *A Historical Guide to Ernest Hemingway* New York: Oxford University Press, Inc., 2000.

MacLeish, Archibald. "His Mirror Was Danger." *Life*, July 14, 1961.

McClane, A.J., ed. *McClane's New Standard Fishing Encyclopedia and International Angling Guide*. New York: Gramercy Books/Random House, 1998.

McIver, Stuart B. *Hemingway's Key West*. Sarasota, Fla.: Pineapple Press, 1993.

McLendon, James. *Papa Hemingway in Key West*. Key West, Fl.: Langley Press, 1972. Revised edition, 1991.

Mellow, James R. *Hemingway: A Life without Consequences*. New York:

Houghton Mifflin Company, 1992.

Migdalski, Edward C., and George S. Fichter. *The Fresh and Salt Water Fishes of the World*. New York: Knopf, 1976; New York: Greenwich House, 1996.

Miller, Linda Patterson, ed. *Letters from the Lost Generation: Gerald and Sara Murphy and Friends*. Gainesville, Fla.: Univ. Press of Florida, 2002.

Miller, Madelaine Hemingway. *Ernie: Hemingway's Sister "Sunny" Remembers*. New York: Crown Publishers, 1975.

Meyers, Jeffrey. *Hemingway: A Biography*. New York: Harper & Row Publishers, 1985.

Oliver, Charles M. *Ernest Hemingway A to Z*. New York: Checkmark Books/ Imprint of Facts on File, Inc., 1999.

Palin, Michael *Hemingway Adventure* New York: St. Martins Press, 1999.

Plath, James, and Frank Simmons. *Remembering Ernest Hemingway*. Key West, Fla.: Ketch and Yawl Press, 1999.

Plimpton, George A., ed. *Ernest Hemingway: The Art of Fiction XXI*. The Paris Review, Inc. Spring 1958.

Reiger, George. *Profiles in Saltwater Angling*. Camden, Me.: Silver Quill Press, 1999.

Reynolds, Michael. *Hemingway: The 1930s*. New York: W. W. Norton and Company, 1997.

Reynolds, Michael. *Hemingway: The Final Years*. New York: W. W. Norton, 1999.

Reynolds, Michael. *Hemingway: The American Homecoming*. Cambridge, Mass.: Blackwell Publishers, 1992.

Ross, Lillian. *Portrait of Hemingway*. New York: The Modern Library/Random House, 1999.

Samuelson, Arnold. *With Hemingway: A Year in Key West and Cuba*. New York: Random House, 1984.

Sandison, Davis. *Ernest Hemingway: An Illustrated Biography*. Chicago: Review Press, Inc., 1998.

Sanford, Marcelline. *At the Hemingways*. Moscow, Idaho: University of Idaho Press, 1999.

Sarusky, Jaime. *Ernest Hemingway and Cojímar*. Habana, Cuba: Jan Corporation, 1991. Photos by Raúl Corrales.

Schaefer, Dave. *Sailing to Hemingway's Cuba*. Dodds Ferry, N.Y.: Sheridan House Inc., 1971.

Scribner, Charles, Jr. *In the Company of Writers*. New York: Charles Scribner's Sons, 1990.

Simmons, Dan. *The Crook Factory*. New York: Avon Books, 1999.

Stanton, Edward F. *Hemingway and Spain: A Pursuit*. Seattle: Univ. of Washington Press, 1989.

Summers, Anthony. *Official and Confidential: The Secret Life of J. Edgar Hoover*. New York: G. P. Putnam's Sons, 1993.

Tessitore, John. *The Hunt and The Feast: A Life of Ernest Hemingway*. New York: Franklin Watts/Division of Grolier Publishing, 1996.

Thomas, Hugh. *Cuba: The Pursuit of Freedom*. New York: Harper & Row Publishers, 1971.

Trogdon, Robert W., ed. *Ernest Hemingway: A Literary Reference*. New York: Carroll & Graff, 1999.

Turnbull, Andrew. *The Letters of F. Scott Fitzgerald*. New York: Charles Scribner's Sons, 1963.

Voss, Frederick. *Picturing Hemingway: A Writer in His Time*. New Haven: Yale Univ. Press, 1999.

Weelack, John Hall. *Editor to Author: The Letters of Maxwell E. Perkins*. Atlanta, Ga.: Cherokee Publishing Co., 1991.

BY ERNEST HEMINGWAY

Baker, Carlos, ed. *Ernest Hemingway: Selected Letters 1917-1961*. New York: Charles Scribner's Sons, 1981.

A Farewell to Arms. New York: Charles Scribner's Sons, 1929; rev. with intro. by Ernest Hemingway, 1948.

Across the River and into the Trees. New York: Charles Scribner's Sons, 1950.

"The Christmas Gift." *Look*, April 20, 1954.

The Complete Short Stories of Ernest Hemingway. New York: Charles Scribner's Sons, 1987.

Death in the Afternoon. New York: Simon & Schuster, 1932.

For Whom the Bell Tolls. New York: Charles Scribner's Sons, 1940.

The Garden of Eden. New York: Simon & Schuster, 1986.

Green Hills of Africa. New York: Charles Scribner's Sons, 1935.

Islands in the Stream. New York: Charles Scribner's Sons, 1970.

The Nick Adams Stories. New York: Charles Scribner's Sons, 1972.

"The Old Man and the Sea." *Life*, September 1, 1952.

The Old Man and the Sea. New York: Charles Scribner's Sons, 1952.

To Have and to Have Not. New York: Charles Scribner's Sons, 1937.

"Visit with Hemingway." *Look*, September 4, 1956.

Hemingway, Sean, ed. *Hemingway on Hunting*. Guilford, Conn.: Lyons Press/Globe Pequot Press, 2001.

Lyons, Nick, ed. *Hemingway on Fishing*. New York: The Lyons Press, 2000.

Phillips, Larry W., ed. *Ernest Hemingway on Writing*. New York: Simon & Schuster, 1984.

White, William, ed. *By-Line: Ernest Hemingway*. New York: Simon & Schuster, 1986.

655

0 2.5km
0 2.5mi

20

Vedado

Nac

Castillo del Príncipe

Plaza de Revoluci

Miramar

Marina Hemingway

Punta de Sotavento

200

Jaimanitas

P l a y a

L a   H a

Marianao

0 1km
0 1mi

Castillo del Morro

Castillo de San Salvador de la Punta

Canal del Puerto

Fortaleza de San Carlos de La Cabaña

Malecón

Museo Nacional de Bellas Artes

Catedral de San Cristóbal

Castillo de la Real Fuerza

Casablanca

La Bodeguita del Medio

La Floridita

Hotel Ambos Mundos

Plaza de San Francisco

Centro

National Capitolio

Basílica Menor de San Francisco de Asís

Havana

La

Plaza Vieja

Habana

Estación Central de Ferrocarriles

Vieja

Bahía de La Habana

Regla

6/03